*HOW TO MAKE YOUR
FIRST QUARTER MILLION
IN REAL ESTATE IN FIVE YEARS*

Also by the Author:

How to Earn Over $50,000 a Year at Home, Parker Publishing Company, Inc.

HOW TO MAKE YOUR FIRST QUARTER MILLION IN REAL ESTATE IN FIVE YEARS

Dan Ramsey

Prentice-Hall, Inc.
Englewood Cliffs, NJ

Prentice-Hall International, Inc., *London*
Prentice-Hall of Australia, Pty., *Sydney*
Prentice-Hall of Canada, Ltd., *Toronto*
Prentice-Hall of India Private Ltd., *New Delhi*
Prentice-Hall of Japan, Inc., *Tokyo*
Prentice-Hall of Southeast Asia Pte. Ltd., *Singapore*
Whitehall Books, Ltd., *Wellington, New Zealand*

© 1979 by

Prentice-Hall, Inc.

Englewood Cliffs, N.J.

All rights reserved. No part of this book may be reproduced in any form or by any means, without permission in writing from the publisher.

Library of Congress Cataloging in Publication Data

Ramsey, Dan
  How to make your first quarter million in real estate in five years.

  Includes index.
  1. Real estate investment. I. Title.
HD1379.R36   332.6'324   79-17084
ISBN 0-13-418350-9

Printed in the United States of America

To my first love—Mom

What This Book Can Do for You

This book can take you step-by-easy-step from wherever you are financially today to a spendable net worth of over $250,000—*a quarter million dollars*—in just a few short years.

In fact, the techniques, ideas and methods you'll learn about in the coming pages can take you to nearly any financial goal—including *one million dollars* or more.

But this book has purposely set an easier goal of a quarter million dollars that the average man and woman with above average dreams can reach in a reasonable time. I know it can be done because as a real estate investment adviser I've assisted others in using the techniques you'll soon learn to reach goals of $250,000, $500,000, $1,000,000 and even $3,000,000 in a few short years.

And they've done it with the easiest to understand, yet most profitable investment opportunity available: buying, upgrading and selling residential income property for profit.

I can't promise you that you'll be a millionaire overnight, but I can show you how you can easily make your first quarter million or more in real estate in a short time.

Here are a few of the real estate wealth techniques you'll learn about in the coming pages:

- The easy-to-follow REAL ESTATE MILLIONAIRE PLAN including the five magical steps that can turn a normal transaction into a gold mine.

- Your WEALTH STAGES—an actual guided tour through each real estate investment phase to show you *exactly* how others have found riches and success with the REAL ESTATE MILLIONAIRE PLAN.
- A full chapter on how to trade your first quarter million for your *first million* with 36 ADVANCED REAL ESTATE INVESTMENT TECHNIQUES.
- PLUS many other profitable ideas and techniques that have been used by many successful Real Estate Millionaires to reach their goals—how to fully protect yourself when buying and selling property, how to negotiate the lowest purchase price and highest sales price, how to turn an orphan property into a rich uncle, how to get bankers to bring money to you, and more.

There's much more. All practical, down-to-earth information that can be used in your first real estate deal—or your fifty-first. And nearly every technique, every step, is backed up with practical examples of how others have made their fortunes in Residential Income real estate:

- How Mark D. bought three brand-new homes with just $12,000 down—all of it borrowed—and *more than doubled* his money the first year.
- How I talked Donna S. into buying her first rental home—which *doubled* her equity *in six months*.
- How Roger and Doris buy older homes, make Selective Improvements, then sell them on contracts for huge profits.
- How Clarence R. purchased his first home with *100% financing* and profited $12,000 in 1½ years.
- And the *complete details* of how Kevin and Dianne S. built Rented Money into more than a *half million dollars* in a few short years.

You're not going to want to put this book down. Once you see people just like yourself—people with jobs, kids, problems and dreams—using my easy-to-understand techniques and methods your mind will race with ideas on how you can go out and do it yourself.

And that's exactly what I want. I want *you* and every other person reading this book to be able to realize your own goals and fill your own life with the success I've found. I want *you* to feel the satisfaction of helping others with their housing needs while you help yourself into a new world of wealth and happiness.

Dan Ramsey

Contents

What This Book Can Do for You 9

1. How to REMAP Your Future with the Real Estate Millionaire Plan 23

    Real Estate: A Game that Anyone Can Play—and Win (24)
    Real Estate Is the World's Best Investment (25)
    Real Estate Is the World's Easiest Investment (25)
    How People Just like You Make More Profits than Large Real Estate Investors (26)
    Making Low Profits the Easy Way (27)
    Earning Higher Profits with Growth Techniques (28)
        How to Make Big Profits with the Six Steps to Wealth (28)
        The Power of Leverage (29)
        How One Investor Built Up Equity (29)
        Making Selective Improvements (30)
        The Art of "Packaging" (30)
        Tax Savings: The Final Step (31)
    The Real Estate Millionaire Plan (31)
    How to Build Your Wealth in Stages (34)
    Turning the Key to Riches with REMAP (35)
        How to Find Your Own Financial Goal (35)

1. **How to REMAP Your Future with the Real Estate Millionaire Plan (cont.)**

    How to Start Your Real Estate Millionaire Plan with Little or No Capital (36)
    The Most Important Ingredient in REMAP (37)
        You Can Buy Your Financial Freedom (38)

2. **How to Find Property with Potential for Earning High Profits** 39

    How to Profit from RI Properties (40)
    Rental Experts Know How to Make Money (41)
    How to Read Growth Trends (41)
    Knowledge is Potential Profit (42)
    Search for and Find Property with Potential (43)
    How to Get Others to Bring Properties with Potential to You (43)
        How to Get the Answers You Want (44)
    Where to Find More Profitable Real Estate Opportunities (45)
        FSBOs Offer a Wealth of PWPs (46)
    Check Properties with Potential for Profitability (47)
        Using CSPs to Check Out a Property (47)
        How to Verify Profitability (48)
        How a Buyer Found a Bargain (49)
    Analyze and Decide about Profitability (50)
    How to Fill Out Your Property Pricing Sheet (51)
    How to Analyze Income and Profitability (51)
    How to Make Even Higher Profits with Residential Income Property (52)

3. **How to Use Imaginative Financing to Find Start-up Money for Real Estate Investing** 57

    Money Breeds Money (58)
    How to Borrow Profitably (58)
    How to Use the Power of Leverage for Profits (59)

CONTENTS

3. **How to Use Imaginative Financing to Find Start-up Money for Real Estate Investing (cont.)**

    How to Get the Loan You Want (60)
    How to Buy Your First Property with Potential Starting with Little or No Cash (61)
    7 Ways to Build Your Breeding Fund (61)
        Using Your Savings (61)
        Sell Real Property (62)
        Sell Personal Property (62)
        Borrow from Your Assets (62)
        Borrow from Tomorrow (62)
        Using the Second Mortgage (63)
        Loan Yourself (63)
    4 Places to Borrow Quick Cash (64)
        Conventional Loans (64)
        Instant Cash (64)
        Other Investors (64)
        Associates (65)
    3 Successful Methods of Starting with No Cash (65)
        100 Percent Financing (65)
        Sweeten the Pot (66)
        Borrow Collateral (66)
    How to Use Conventional Financing to REMAP Your Future (67)
    How to Secure Your Conventional Financing (68)
        Using Loan-to-Value Ratios (68)
        How Lenders Manipulate Investors for Profit (69)
    Financing Secrets Used by Real Estate Millionaires (69)
        Why Sellers Pay Points on FHA and VA Loans (70)
    How to Build Your Fortune with Imaginative Financing (71)
        Pay-off Methods (72)
    How Second Mortgages Are Used by the Real Estate Pros (72)
        Why Smart Investors Use Assumptions (73)

4. **How to Use Creative Purchasing to Negotiate Profitable Real Estate Transactions** 75

    How to Take the Wind Out of Real Estate Risk (76)
        Crossroad Risks (76)
        Using the Plus and Minus Sheet (77)
        How to Overcome the Minuses (78)
    How to Make Your Offer on Property with Potential (79)
        The Importance of Legal Descriptions (79)
        Price and Terms (80)
        Escrow Instructions (80)
        Getting Your Earnest Money (81)
    How to Write Your Own Terms (81)
    How to Present Your Offer to the Seller (84)
        Presenting an Offer to Ensure Acceptance (86)
    How to Negotiate a Profitable Deal (86)
        How to Successfully Handle an Owner's Counter Offer (87)
        The See-Saw Negotiating Techniques (87)
    How to Close Your Transaction Profitably (88)
    How to Close in Escrow (89)

5. **How to Accelerate Equities for Higher Real Estate Profits** 91

    Finding Profitable Renters (92)
    How to Initiate Renters to Your Rules (94)
    How to Keep Rentals Profitable (96)
        The Income Method (96)
        The Market Data Method (97)
        The Cost Method (98)
    How to Keep Expenses Down (98)
        Keeping Management Costs Down (98)
        Planning Ahead for Maintenance (99)
        Cutting Vacancy Losses to Zero (99)
    How to Handle Problems (100)

CONTENTS

5. **How to Accelerate Equities for Higher Real Estate Profits (cont.)**

   How to Make Selective Improvements (101)
   How to Selectively Improve the Yard (101)
   How to Selectively Improve the Interior of Your Residential Income Property (102)
   How to Profit from Other Accelerated Equity Techniques (103)
   How to Depreciate Your Property for Extra Profits (104)
   How to Accelerate Your Equity with Equity Payoff (105)
   Making Higher Profits with Packaging (106)
       Manny V. Uses Productive Marketing Techniques (106)

6. **How to Add to Your Real Estate Profits with Productive Marketing** 109

   How to Cash in Your Chips (110)
       Deciding on Productive Marketing (111)
   How to Sell Your RI Property Profitably (111)
       Income Opportunity Fact Sheet (112)
   How to Sell on the Best Terms (113)
       The "Cash" Method (113)
       The Wrap-Around Method (114)
       The Soft Money Mortgage (115)
   How to Refinance Your Property Profitably (116)
       How to Set Up Conventional Financing (116)
   How to Profit from Tax Planning (117)
       Taking Title (118)
   Tax Considerations on Operation (120)
   Tax Considerations on Termination (121)
   Delaying Your Tax Obligation (122)
   The Real Estate Millionaire Plan Will Take You to Your Goal (123)

7. Using Leverage in SFRs as Real Estate Profit
   Starting Blocks 125

   Building Your Real Estate Fortune in Wealth Stages
     (126)
   How One Young Couple Developed Their Real Estate Millionaire Plan into Wealth Stages (126)
   Getting Your Fortune Started Today (127)
   Wealth Stage 1 (128)
   How to Choose Your First SFR (129)
   How the Simpsons Find Their First Profitable Property with Potential (129)
   Checking Out Property with Potential to Ensure the
     Best Investment (130)
   Using an SFR Investment Rating Guide to Find the
     Best Property with Potential (131)
   How One Investor Used the SFR Investment Rating
     Guide (132)
   Imaginative Financing and the Power of Leverage
     (133)
   Making Big Money with Leverage Ratios (133)
   How the Simpsons Used Leverage Ratios to Find the
     Most Profitable Opportunity (134)
   Using Creative Purchasing Techniques to Ensure a
     Profit on Your First SFR (135)
   How a Country Boy Made Big Money in the City
     (136)
   How Kevin and Dianne Used Creative Purchasing to
     Make an Offer on Their PWP (137)
   Activating Your Alternative Plan (138)
   Making Selective Improvements on Your First SFR to
     Accelerate Equity (139)
   These Investors Build Equity from the First Day (139)
   How to Handle Ad Calls and Find the Best Tenants
     (140)
   How to Check Out Potential Tenants (141)
   Using Productive Marketing to Increase Wealth Stage
     1 Profits (142)
   The Simpsons Reach Their First Wealth Stage Goal
     (143)

CONTENTS

8. Building Equity in SFRs with High Powered Real Estate Investment Techniques 145

   Finding More Properties with Potential for Earning Substantial Profits (146)
   How These Smart Investors Learned Profit Secrets by Reviewing Wealth Stage 1 (147)
   How Don C. Found Five Properties with Potential (148)
   Inspecting SFRs for Profitability (149)
   Making a Decision on the Best SFRs (150)
   Making Imaginative Financing Work for You with a Creative Wrap-Around Mortgage (151)
   Kevin and Dianne Use a Wrap-Around to Creatively Purchase Two Profitable Units (151)
   How to Use Preapproved Financing and Buy like Cash (152)
   These Investors Make $5,000 with Imaginative Financing (153)
   How to Multiply Profits with a Gross Rent Multiplier (153)
   Putting Your GRM into Action (154)
   How to Turn Quick Dollars with Easy SIs (154)
   The Simpsons Turn Cosmetics into Cash (155)
   Cashing in on Accelerated Equity (156)
   How Two Investors Refinanced for Quick Cash (157)
   How the Simpsons Make Big Profits Selling SFR-2 and -3 (158)

9. Switching to MFDs to Increase Income and Lower Expenses 161

   MFDs—The Most Profitable RI Properties (161)
      Higher Income (162)
      MFDs Offer Lower Expenses (163)
      Better Cash Flow (163)
      Tax Shelter (164)
      Controlled Risks (164)
      Equity Growth (164)

9. **Switching to MFDs to Increase Income and Lower Expenses (cont.)**

    The Smartest Investors Use This Formula (165)
        Cap Rates and Rent (165)
    How to Find an MFD Property with Potential (166)
    Searching for Your First Profitable MFD (167)
        Reconsidering the Opportunities (168)
    How Imaginative Financing Can Turn the Key on Your First MFD (168)
    Smart Money Techniques for Negotiating a Creative Purchase (169)
    Using Advanced Creative Purchasing Techniques to Negotiate a Profitable Transaction (171)
    Setting a GRM for Your MFD (172)
    Using Your New GRM to Make Substantial Profits (172)
    How to Keep Uncle Sam Out of Your Pocket (173)
    How to Tally Your Profits from Wealth Stage 3 (174)

10. **Increasing Your Net Worth with Accelerated Equity Techniques** 177

    How Smart Real Estate Investors Trim These Two Major Costs (178)
    Build Your Bank Account by Cutting Vacancy Costs (178)
    Save Thousands of Dollars Every Year by Cutting Management Costs (179)
    How to Sell Now—Pay Taxes Later (181)
    How the Simpsons Exchange Equities Profitably (181)
    Comparing Exchanges Profitably (182)
    Working Out the Terms of a Tax Deferred Exchange (183)
    How to Use a Profitability Checklist (183)
    How Ray B. Saved Thousands of Dollars (185)
    Taking Over a $400,000 MFD (185)
    Setting Profitable Tenant Guidelines (186)
    Cashing In with Productive Marketing (187)
    How Kevin and Dianne Refinance Their MFD (188)

CONTENTS

11. Reaching Your Financial Goal with the Real Estate Millionaire Plan.. 191

    How Successful Investors Find Property with Potential (191)
    Using the Telephone to Pick Up Big Opportunities (192)
    How a Smart Investor Can Use Imaginative Financing to Pick Up Bargains (194)
    How Two Investors Turn a Failure into Success (194)
    Making Sure an Opportunity Isn't a Red Herring (195)
    Using Imaginative Financing to Put Together a Profitable Opportunity (195)
    Using Productive Marketing Techniques to Accelerate Equity (196)
    Crossing the Finish Line (198)

12. How to Use Advanced Techniques to Make Your First Million in Real Estate in Ten Years 201

    How to Cash in on the Real Estate Millionaire Plan (202)
    How to Trade Accelerated Equity for More Equity (202)
    How to Trade Accelerated Equity for Cash (203)
    How to Trade Accelerated Equity for Annuity (203)
    How to use Advanced Real Estate Investment Techniques to Build Your Fortune to a Million Dollars (204)
    Advanced Real Estate Investment Techniques for Finding Property with Potential (205)
    Advanced Real Estate Investment Techniques for Using Imaginative Financing (208)
    Advanced Real Estate Investment Techniques for Using Creative Purchasing (211)
    Advanced Real Estate Investment Techniques to Accelerate Equities for Higher Profits (213)
    Advanced Real Estate Investment Techniques to Add to Your Profits with Productive Marketing (214)

12. How to Use Advanced Techniques to Make Your First Million in Real Estate in Ten Years (cont.)

    Other Profitable Applications of the Real Estate Millionaire Plan (217)
    How Sylvan C. Sat Back and Made Money with REMAP (217)
    How Bill H. Built His Fortune at Home (218)
    How Chet R. Became a Millionaire Handyman (218)
    The End of the Beginning (219)

Index 221

1

How to Remap Your Future with the Real Estate Millionaire Plan

> "Ninety percent of all millionaires become so through owning real estate. More money has been made in real estate than in all industrial investments combined. The wise young man or wage earner invests his money in real estate."
>
> —Andrew Carnegie
> Multimillionaire industrialist

It's a fact! There have been vastly more millionaires made with real estate in the past few decades than in any other field. These millions of spendable dollars weren't made by people who sacrificed everything they had and worked at their investments 24 hours a day for dozens of years. More real estate fortunes have been made by people who started on a part-time basis with little more than a goal, a simple plan and rented money. People just like you.

And for every real estate investor that made a million dollars there have been thousands of others who made a half million or a quarter million or some other figure that helped them enjoy life a little better while helping others with a very basic need.

There are hundreds of variations and specialized methods of building real estate millionaires out of otherwise average people, but each of these systems is based on the same handful of rules. As a professional real estate investment advisor, I've helped many people understand and use these basic investment rules to bring them more wealth than they could have found anywhere else. I'm going to do the same for you.

How to Make Your First Quarter Million in Real Estate in Five Years will outline the basic steps to profitable real estate ownership, plus offer one of the safest and most reliable methods of reaching a net worth of $250,000 or more in just five short years. This book isn't a get-rich-quick scheme based on luck and highly sophisticated skill. Rather, it's a book of easy-to-follow steps and clear examples that will show you how to open your own doors of opportunity to a world of wealth and prosperity—a world in which you belong.

Real Estate: A Game that Anyone Can Play—and Win

Real estate and its associated services is one of the nation's largest industries. In fact, the total value of real estate in the United States is now over $3,000,000,000,000—three *trillion* dollars. That's about 65 percent of this nation's wealth.

And real estate changes hands often. Over four million pieces of property are bought and sold each year. Most at a healthy profit.

The major part of this industry of real estate is done by brokers who help families, investors and corporations buy and sell everything from two bedroom homes and vacation retreats to apartment complexes, shopping centers and huge office buildings.

Other partners in the wealth of real estate include construction companies, banks, savings and loan associations, credit unions and mortgage companies, property management firms, appraisal firms and the many government agencies that assist the housing and real estate industry. They include the Federal Housing Administration (FHA), Housing and Urban Development (HUD), Veterans Administration (VA), Farmers Home Administration (FmHA) and federal banking agencies.

Real Estate Is the World's Best Investment

Why is real estate such a big business?

Because it's a prime necessity. People must have shelter. If people had to, they could do without dry cleaners, landscaping services, taco stands and car washes. But they must always have shelter. The rent or house payment is made first and the rest of the money goes for car washes, cleaning bills and tacos.

Real estate is a prime necessity because it offers:

- Shelter—a place out of the rain, sun, snow and wind. It should offer shelter from other people.

- Location—it should be situated close to other necessities: food and shopping, schools, work and recreation.

- Amenities or extras—once the basics of shelter and location are satisfied people buy or rent real estate for the extras: extra bedrooms, carpeting, a second bathroom, double garage and family room. The "basic" home in America has grown in the last two decades from about 900 square feet to nearly 1200 square feet because of our "need" for extras.

Real Estate Is the World's Easiest Investment

You've lived in houses or apartments all of your life. You understand firsthand what people want in a living unit. You've rented, leased or even purchased your own unit—and have probably lived in many others.

In other words, you have at least *some* firsthand knowledge of residential real estate. This knowledge can make you many thousands of dollars in profits as you consider what others are looking for and decide how best to bring it to them. So real estate is not new to you. You've been around it and used it all of your life.

Another reason why real estate is a good investment for the beginning investor is the availability of information. With the facts you'll learn in the next chapter, you'll know how to gather profit-making information on nearly any parcel of land or house in the nation. You'll find out how to easily discover the lot size, square footage, type of deed and ownership, taxes, valuation and even the property's income and market value. You'll learn how to search public records for the best buys.

How People Just like You Make More Profits than Large Real Estate Investors

One of the best things about real estate investments is that you can start small and build as you learn. Your initial investment can be a few thousand dollars or—as you will learn in coming chapters—none of your own money.

In fact, the average person can make high profits in real estate when huge investment corporations can't. Why?

Because you have developed a working knowledge of *local* real estate conditions and situations—and you can quickly take advantage of them. While million dollar corporations are delegating research staff members to the job of analyzing a possible purchase, you as an individual can quickly research and decide whether it's a profitable deal and take appropriate action. *You* can move more quickly than an overweight corporation.

You are also more interested in the outcome of a purchase than a 9-to-5 employee of a professional real estate investment firm. To them it's just another "acquisition," but to you it's a highly profitable opportunity. You have the distinct advantage over these large firms.

So you, as an individual investor, have more avenues of profit opportunity open to you than the large real estate investment corporations. And you can move quickly with more assurance because of your knowledge and size advantage. This book will show you how to develop—and profit—from these advantages.

Making Low Risk Profits the Easy Way

You can invest in all types of real estate: residential income, commercial, industrial, agricultural, mining and raw land. As you're beginning to learn, the easiest, most profitable and least risky venture for the beginning investor is residential income. Residential income property (RI) is simply any real estate that people will pay you to live in. It's single family residences (SFRs) and multi-family dwellings (MFDs).

In searching for your first real estate investment, you'll probably be most interested in:

- Safety—finding properties that are low risk which means your investment is safe from loss.
- Growth—locating properties that will allow you to use a small investment to earn a healthy profit.

Residential income properties (RIs) can offer you safety or low risk because their purchase, operation and sale are easy for the beginner to understand and control. RIs are also anti-inflationary and offer liquidity or ready cash.

We've already discussed the first point: safety because you are familiar with RI properties as a homeowner and/or apartment renter. You understand firsthand what renters want and need to remain happy and profitable for you. And because of this understanding RIs are easier to control than complex commercial and industrial properties.

One of the greatest investment features about RIs is that they are anti-inflationary and anti-depressionary. In other words, real estate values always rise with inflation and values tend not to drop during recession or depression times. They are always on the increase—and always at a rate faster than inflation. There are few investments that hold their prices as well during unstable economic times. Why? Again, because residential real estate is a necessity of life.

RI property offers one more safety feature important to the

first-time investor: it is liquid. In other words, residential income property is easy to sell or borrow against when you need ready cash.

As an example, if you found a prime opportunity tomorrow to turn 200 percent on an investment of $10,000 within six months—but all of your cash was tied up in real estate—it would be much easier to sell or mortgage your RI house or apartment units than to sell or mortgage a shopping center, industrial complex or farm.

Earning Higher Profits with Growth Techniques

Most important to the investor, RI property offers *growth*. With RIs you can easily take a small amount of money, use the principle of leverage you'll soon learn more about and build your net worth by 100 percent, 200 percent and more each and every year. This investment growth comes from many different sources in real estate—and the more growth sources an investment offers, the faster it will grow and the safer it will be from loss.

How to Make Big Profits with the Six Steps to Wealth

Residential income properties offer financial growth through the *Six Steps to Growth:*

- Leverage
- Equity build-up
- Appreciation
- Selective improvements
- Packaging
- Tax savings

Leverage is the principle of physics that says you can move a heavy object by placing a lever under something you want moved, on top of a second object—or fulcrum—and applying pressure to the opposite end of the lever. A small amount of force on one end of the lever transfers a larger force to the other end and, hopefully, moves the heavy object.

Applied to real estate and finance, you can gain tremendous leverage or power from your dollars by using the fulcrum of Rented

HOW TO REMAP YOUR FUTURE

Money to move or purchase a property. Leverage *multiplies* your buying power—and your profits.

Let's see how Gene W. used the Six Steps to Growth listed above in the purchase and profit-making of his first residential income property.

The Power of Leverage

With the power of leverage Gene purchased a brand new home from the builder for $27,000 on a real estate contract. The terms were $1,500 down and $215 a month for 30 years. This was a couple of years ago. Today, Gene's RI is worth $41,000. That's a total increase in value of about 25 percent a year. More important, that's over an *1100 percent* increase in two years on Gene's initial investment.

Where did this huge profit come from? From the Six Steps to Growth.

As explained, leverage gave Gene the opportunity to buy his first RI with an initial investment of about six cents on the dollar. Not all leverage opportunities are this good, but with the techniques you'll be learning about in coming chapters you'll find them more common than you think.

How One Investor Built Up Equity

Gene also earned profits from what I call Equity Build-up. Gene rented his home at $225 per month the first year. With payments of $215 plus taxes and insurance he had what is called a negative cash flow. In other words his expenses were more than his income. How did he profit from this situation? His renters were paying off his debt on the home. The first year he lost a few dollars because of negative cash flow, but made many times more because the balance on his mortgage went down by nearly $1,000.

Just a side note: Gene increased rents the second year to $250 a month and had a positive cash flow (more income than expenses) that gave him back his few dollars a month. More on positive and negative cash flow later.

Gene W.'s best profits came from Appreciation, or the increase in value the home earned due to inflation and demand. In Gene's area homes were going up a conservative 15 percent a year. That's $4,000 to $5,000 a year in no-work profits.

Making Selective Improvements

Gene made a $2,000 profit from Selective Improvements. Gene learned—as you will—that high profits can be earned in both new and older homes with what many RI owners call "Dress Up" or "Cosmetics." In the case of an older home it's a matter of painting inside and out, replacing kitchen counter tops, modernizing cabinets and plumbing and landscaping. Even a new home requires cosmetics. Gene's home was brand new and needed landscaping. For a couple of hundred dollars in seed and bushes, Gene increased the value of his new property about $2,500. A couple of weekends after he purchased it, his new RI was worth $29,500—because he knew how to build extra profits with Selective Improvements.

The Art of "Packaging"

Packaging is similar to physical cosmetics for a home in that it increases the value of a property because of the ease and convenience of ownership. Packaging is a matter of making a property easy to buy. Gene decided to hold his property awhile longer, but his purchase of the home in the first place offers a good example of Packaging. The builder used two Packaging methods: brokerage and terms.

The builder of Gene's RI property hired a broker to help him sell his house. He was willing to pay a commission to the broker for taking the problem of advertising, showing, qualifying buyers and handling the volumes of paperwork involved in the sale of a home. Broker Packaging made the home easier to sell and easier to buy.

The second thing the builder did to Package his property was to offer it on excellent terms. The down payment covered the broker's fees so the builder didn't really get any cash in his pocket at the time of the sale. But he did get a contract from the purchaser that said he would pay the builder $215 a month for 30 years. The builder's loan with the bank to build the home was for $20,000 at $160 a month. Rather than take a cash profit at closing, the builder decided to Package his property to make it easier for the buyer to buy. For this

Packaging he earned the *interest* on his $5,500 profit for 30 years—$14,300!

Tax Savings: The Final Step

The final step to growth in RI properties is tax savings. Even though properties appreciate or rise in value each year due to demand and increasing replacement costs, the tax man allows you to depreciate—or deduct value for aging—your income property. I'll get further into the kinds of depreciation and how you can take advantage of this very legal tax loophole in a later chapter. Right now I'll tell you that Gene W. was able to save $400 a year in hard earned cash tax savings because of two tax "loopholes": depreciation and interest payments. Besides depreciation, tax laws state that you can fully deduct as an expense any interest you must pay on a mortgage. When Gene started making payments to the builder, he found that more than three-quarters of those payments was interest and less than a quarter went to the principal. Later this ratio will change, but during the first two years Gene saved a total of over $800 in taxes because of these two tax rules. You'll be learning more about them.

Investing in residential income properties, SFRs and MFDs (single family residences and multi-family dwellings), offers you the safety of low risk and easy management, plus the six different methods of financial growth. I hope that you can now see that the *best* way to earn your fortune is through owning residential income real estate. Now you are going to be shown how to buy your own financial independence.

The Real Estate Millionaire Plan

Whether your financial goal is a quarter million, half million, a million dollars or more, you will be able to apply my REAL ESTATE MILLIONAIRE PLAN compiled from the success secrets of hundreds of otherwise average people who have made a million dollars or more in real estate.

The REAL ESTATE MILLION-AIRE PLAN (REMAP) is not a pie-in-the-sky, get-rich-quick scheme. It's a down-to-earth plan that offers not only an attainable goal, but also a proven method that has brought substantial wealth to thousands of others.

REMAP is based on the best investment you can make—an investment that has made more millionaires than any other—residential real estate. Investments are as safe as you make them. Growth is as quick as you desire. Control of your investment is as strong as you wish.

REMAP offers safety for your investment dollar because it is secured by an asset that cannot be easily stolen, depleted or hidden. It's a prime necessity of life. And as our roller coaster economy moves from depression to inflation and back again, real estate investments follow the high side of the economic curve to bring profits in any type of market.

REMAP offers growth. It gives you the power of leverage to build a fortune with a small starting capital. Few investments can match the leverage available to the real estate investor. And leverage is the key to *multiplying profits*. If your property increases in value 12 percent in one year and you purchased it with an initial investment of only 10 percent, you are actually making *120 percent profit* on your initial investment. That's the Power of Leverage.

REMAP offers you control. Your stock market investments soar and plummet uncontrolled by you. Investing in the stock market is a matter of learning when to jump on—and jump off—the roller coaster. But real estate profits are much more controllable.

The REAL ESTATE MILLIONAIRE PLAN is the *best* way to REMAP your financial future.

The REAL ESTATE MILLIONAIRE PLAN is a proven step-by-step system for finding, negotiating, buying, operating and profiting from the ownership of residential income real estate.

The REAL ESTATE MILLIONAIRE PLAN is an easy-to-follow system of building your wealth with a simple investment formula:

$$PWP \times IF + CP \times AE + PM = SP$$

Or, PROPERTY WITH POTENTIAL MULTIPLIED BY IMAGINATIVE FINANCING PLUS CREATIVE PURCHASING MULTIPLIED BY ACCELERATED EQUITY PLUS PRODUCTIVE MARKETING EQUALS SUBSTANTIAL PROFITS.

HOW TO REMAP YOUR FUTURE

Let's see how the REAL ESTATE MILLIONAIRE PLAN works.

REMAP STEP 1: Property with Potential (PWP). The first step in my profit-making formula is finding a unit of real estate that has the potential for making you a sizeable profit. It's learning the ins and outs of finding and recognizing a real estate investment opportunity. It's finding out what a good investment looks like, searching for it, recognizing it, then starting the steps to profit from it. It's being a profit detective.

REMAP STEP 2: Imaginative Financing (IF) is learning how to find Rented Money at one rate that you can use to earn a much higher interest rate. IF combines conventional financing with unconventional or creative financing to show you how to purchase and profit with other people's money.

REMAP STEP 3: Creative Purchasing (CP) is learning how to buy properties for the best price, on the best terms. It's negotiating a profitable deal. It's learning how to take title for safety and tax savings. CP is learning how to use real estate agents and escrow companies to your best advantage. It's learning how to make money before you buy.

REMAP STEP 4: Accelerated Equity (AE). As you've learned, the passing of time will give you profit growth through equity build-up (or mortgage pay-off), normal appreciation and tax savings. Then there are the even better profits you can earn from Accelerated Equity. AE is learning how to find, make and profit from Selective Improvements made to residential income properties. You'll learn how to keep units rented, handle renters profitably, increase rents and keep expenses down. You'll learn how to quicken your profits with the dozens of fortune-building ideas.

REMAP STEP 5: Productive Marketing (PM). The final step in the REAL ESTATE MILLIONAIRE PLAN shows you exactly how to build extra value—and profits—in your property through packaging, promoting and profitably selling it for the highest dollar—*plus* offers you *extra* savings through smart tax planning.

The REMAP Formula can be profitably applied to any real estate opportunity. Write it down and carry it with you. Review it daily. This easy-to-remember formula can quickly help you decide whether an opportunity will bring you closer to your own financial goal. The REMAP System will show you the way.

How to Build Your Wealth in Stages

The easiest way to build anything worthwhile is step-by-step. To build a house you must first build a foundation, then build the walls, then the roof, and so on.

Your wealth, too, must be built in stages. First you build your starting fund, then you invest it to build your equity higher and higher until you've reached your own goal.

In the second half of this book you'll watch a very average couple invest their money and skills in residential income real estate for *profit*. You'll follow them step-by-step through their own WEALTH STAGES as they buy, accelerate and profit from each of their properties—from houses to apartment complexes. You'll see just how easy it is to profitably apply the REAL ESTATE MILLIONAIRE PLAN to residential income real estate on a part-time basis.

Kevin and Dianne Simpson used the REAL ESTATE MILLIONAIRE PLAN to reach their personal financial goal in five WEALTH STAGES.

WEALTH STAGE 1. You'll see Kevin and Dianne search for and buy their first RI investment—a single family residence or SFR—with Rented Money. You'll watch them use the Power of Leverage and the REMAP formula to *double their equity* in twelve months.

WEALTH STAGE 2. Then you'll follow the Simpsons every step of the way as they use REMAP to purchase more SFRs and build their equity even faster. You'll see them use Accelerated Equity techniques to turn good profits into Substantial Profits, then you'll watch them profitably sell some of their equity to build their pyramid even higher.

WEALTH STAGE 3. You'll be there when Kevin and Dianne use their skills learned with SFRs to branch out into profitable multi-family dwellings or MFDs. You'll watch them apply advanced techniques of the REMAP formula to *double their equity again*.

WEALTH STAGE 4. The Simpsons will show you exactly how they use the Power of Leverage and the REAL ESTATE MILLIONAIRE PLAN to continue to build their equity to over *$128,000* with MFDs.

WEALTH STAGE 5. You will see these typical investors find Property with Potential, use Imaginative Financing, buy with Creative Purchasing methods, build with Accelerated Equity techniques and turn it all into their final goal of over a *quarter million dollars* with Productive Marketing.

You may set up four WEALTH STAGES, or six or ten to reach your own financial goal, but you'll go beyond theory and learn from actual examples as you follow the Simpsons reach their goal of making their first quarter million in real estate in five years.

Turning the Key to Riches with REMAP

The REMAP formula of turning opportunities into profits is only part of the REAL ESTATE MILLIONAIRE PLAN. The other part—just as important—is the goal-setting and planning of your own WEALTH STAGES. There are hundreds of people who know and understand the REMAP concept, but who cannot really reach higher than they are right now because they don't know where they want to reach. They have no long- and short-range goals.

How to Find Your Own Financial Goal

Everything today has a price. Some prices are clearly stated in terms of money while others are more vague in terms of knowledge, skill or time. Some prices must be paid in all of these commodities. And by now you've probably discovered that life's key is deciding what you want, finding out what the price tag is, deciding whether the price is worth it, then acting on your decision.

My goal—and maybe yours, too—is financial independence. I've learned that I really can't buy "happiness," but that I can enjoy the search for it when I am completely free of my financial obligations to myself and my family to provide all the necessities and a few of the luxuries on a regular basis.

In other words, if I didn't have to concentrate so hard on making a living I could enjoy these days much more. So my goal is to be financially independent—to use concentrated time, knowledge, skill and money to:

- Rid myself of the worry of how to provide for my needs and basic wants today and tomorrow, and
- Free more of the 24 hours a day I've been given in order to continue my exploration of life's pleasures.

What's the price of this goal? For each of us the price is different. Some will only have to pay $100,000 for their lifetime financial independence. Others might have to pay $250,000, $500,000, $1,000,000 or more. An equity of $250,000 reinvested into an annuity, an investment that pays you back in monthly installments, will pay you $2,000 *a month for 30 years.* Is this goal worth the price you'll have to pay working part-time for a few years at an enjoyable and profitable investment?

You know what you want. You know what the price is. You've made the decision to pay the small price in order to get something of greater value. Now it's time to act.

How to Start Your Real Estate Millionaire Plan with Little or No Capital

You can start your WEALTH STAGES with as little cash as you wish. The REAL ESTATE MILLIONAIRE PLAN offers you ideas and methods of building your fortune with little or no capital and building it into a quarter million dollars or more in five years, three years or any timetable you set.

Here's the plan that the Simpson's use later in this book. They decided to build $8,000 into $250,000 in five years by *doubling their equity* each year with the REAL ESTATE MILLIONAIRE PLAN. They made each WEALTH STAGE a year long and set

HOW TO REMAP YOUR FUTURE

these approximate financial goals for each of their five WEALTH STAGES:

WEALTH STAGE	STARTING CAPITAL	ENDING CAPITAL
1	$8,000	$16,000
2	$16,000	$32,000
3	$32,000	$64,000
4	$64,000	$128,000
5	$128,000	$256,000

By building their wealth in stages, the Simpson's goal was not the seemingly difficult one of earning a net worth of over $250,000 in five years, but just to *double their net worth each year for five years*. So their first year's goal—WEALTH STAGE 1—was to turn $8,000 into $16,000.

But you don't have to start with $8,000 as the Simpsons did. I'm going to show you exactly how to begin your WEALTH STAGES with little or no capital and still build your equity to more than $16,000 during your first WEALTH STAGE.

You'll learn the techniques of Imaginative Financing and how to raise capital within days, how to build your own real estate fortune with just your signature and how to take advantage of the smart financing techniques used by real estate millionaires in Chapter 3.

The Most Important Ingredient in REMAP

Maybe you've made a few financial mistakes in your lifetime. Maybe you've had a business that didn't work out. Maybe you've had problems with investments in the past. I'm going to ask you to put it all behind you. Past failures do not apply. Your road to success is cleared. The way is well marked. Others have gone ahead and are willing to show you the way. Suspend your disbelief and let your desire to succeed take over. You *will* succeed with the REAL ESTATE MILLIONAIRE PLAN.

You will also need a willingness to learn new things. I'm satisfied that you have this quality—or you wouldn't be trying to improve your situation by buying and reading this book.

You will have to take calculated risks. You know that. But you also know that there's a world of difference between *risk* and *calculated risk*. Risk is trying to fly a plane when you've never had practice or instruction. Calculated risk is like climbing in your car and driving to work. You are comfortable with your vehicle and you know the road. You have the reflexes and skill to avoid collisions. You *are* risking your life, but it's a calculated risk—and well worth the goal.

Finally, to really succeed you must be willing to look into the future and decide exactly what you want from it. You must see yourself enjoying the things you wish to earn. You must have goals and they must be vivid.

You Can Buy Your Financial Freedom

In other words, the REAL ESTATE MILLIONAIRE PLAN is not a free ride. It's going to take some work, some time and some money. But you can clearly see that the price you will be paying is very small compared to what you will be receiving: financial independence. Enough financial independence to *buy your freedom* and spend the rest of your life doing the things you've always wanted to do—with the people you've always wanted to do them with.

Enough talk. Let's get right into finding your first Property with Potential using my REAL ESTATE MILLIONAIRE PLAN.

2

How to Find Property with Potential for Earning High Profits

Making money is similar to making a cake. You can throw a handful of ingredients together and hope they somehow turn themselves into a delicious cake—or you can read the directions on how others have made good cakes, do exactly what they did and confidently expect the same results.

Your recipe for finding Property with Potential is a tested and proven method handed down from millionaire to entrepreneur. It has five basic ingredients:

- LEARN exactly how real estate profits are made.
- SEARCH for the properties that fit these requirements and help you complete your financial goals.
- CHECK each potential purchase to authenticate facts and figures.
- ANALYZE each real estate opportunity.
- DECIDE on the best action to take.

How to Profit from RI Properties

Renters rent because they don't want to invest their time or money on a long term basis. They don't want to tie up their capital on a down payment or their weekends on maintenance and improvement. Renters would rather pay someone else to do these things than pay themselves.

Offer them what they're looking for and they'll pay you.

What do renters look for in a living unit? The same three things you should look for when you're considering the purchase of a profitable rental property:

> SHELTER—Renters, like anyone else, need a place to sleep, eat, relax and play. They prefer a basic home with few extras—and they pay rents accordingly.
>
> LOCATION—Most renters prefer to be near jobs, recreation, shopping and transportation. Rentals located conveniently near these services traditionally have less vacancies and command a better rent.
>
> PRICE—Renters normally pay between 20 and 30 percent of their monthly gross income on rent. Your rentals should be priced within this range for the average worker in your area.

Preston W. found what he thought was a great buy. It was a large new home in a prestige neighborhood on excellent terms. It was priced about $15,000 over what the average rental homes were costing, but the low down payment was attractive so Preston decided to buy it as a rental unit.

In doing so Preston broke all three rules of good rentals: he bought a home that was larger than most renters would need; it was located away from jobs and shopping; and it had to rent for $100 more than typical rentals in his city. His rental unit sat vacant seven months out of the first year he owned it. Preston has since sold it and traded his equity for a smaller and more basic rental closer to jobs and services that rents below the average market. It stays rented all year.

Rental Experts Know How to Make Money

You're on your way to becoming a Rental Expert. You'll soon know a great deal about your local rental market, how many units are available, how many renters there are, what price units are renting for, what basic building and zoning rules are—and you'll learn how to turn all of this information into a healthy profit.

Step One: to find out how large the rental market is in your area check the "For Rent" section of your local daily newspaper. Follow it each day as closely as others follow the stock market pages. Decide what ads stay in for long periods, which ones seem to move fast and what features these rentals have. Also call a few ads to see how others handle renters.

The classifieds will also tell you what landlords are getting for their rental units. Later I'll give you some methods of setting your own rentals, but right now the best price to charge is 10 percent *less* than the average rent on similar units. You'll easily save that much each year on vacancies and turn-over.

Another thing you can do to become a Rental Expert is visit your local courthouse and ask about local zoning and planning. What type of zoning is required for apartments and duplexes? What are local building codes? What directions do the city planners see as the growth directions? Why? A few hours with area planners can make you thousands of easy dollars over the years.

How to Read Growth Trends

Renters are usually only looking six months or a year ahead. As a Rental Expert you must look farther into the future. You must see how an area will grow and develop and what effect that action will have on your properties. Remember, you're looking for Property with *Potential*.

For over half a century growth has been from the farm to the city. For the past 20 years there has been a backwash of movement from the city to the suburbs. Property in the suburbs has increased in value sometimes twice as fast as city property. You can profit from this trend.

Donna M. was a secretary. Through her job she heard about a new electronics firm coming into her town. Reading this economic trend, Donna used $3,000 of her savings as a down payment on a rental near the proposed site. Within a year economic growth had turned Donna's $3,000 into $12,000. Today Donna has eighteen rentals and employs her own secretary.

Burton L. made money with a map. After hearing the *Basic Rule of Growth* that the fastest growth lies in a direct line between the downtown area and the city's best neighborhood, Burton drew such a line on his local map. After further study Burton and two partners purchased land and built an apartment complex near that line. Sure enough, their investment grew at a rate nearly *twice* that of similar complexes in other parts of the same city.

Donna M. and Burton L. learned how to keep their eyes open as Rental Experts and take advantage of economic and directional trends to earn substantial profits.

Knowledge is Potential Profit

You can profit from nearly everything you learn, but knowledge isn't profit, it's *potential* profit. In other words, you can potentially turn knowledge into profit. The fact that a new electronics firm was coming to Donna M.'s town was knowledge, but it wasn't profit until Donna did something about it. Donna had to learn, search, check, analyze and decide.

And that's what you must do. You must search out ideas and information and *use* that knowledge in order to make a profit.

In fact, the same idea can be applied to reading this book. In its pages are the ideas and information gleaned from hundreds of real estate success stories. But as it sits here on these pages it is only knowledge. It needs one more ingredient to make these ideas profitable—*you.*

Search for and Find Property with Potential

As you've learned, Property with Potential for profits must offer the renter basic shelter, convenient location and reasonable price. You've also studied your own rental market and found what other rentals are available, how much rent is being charged and what location most rentals are in.

It's time to look at your own needs as an investor.

Your first requirement is to find a property that you can purchase with the cash or equity you have available. Later in the REAL ESTATE MILLIONAIRE PLAN you'll be buying and selling six-figure properties, but starting out your capital assets are $8,000 or less. You'll want to use as much leverage as possible.

Your second requirement is to find a property that can offer you a good return on your investment. You'll look for a property that can increase in value with the *Six Steps to Growth* while offering renters enough value to keep your units full.

Where can you find these Properties with Potential?

Some property owners will come to you because of newspaper ads or other contacts you've made. These sellers are usually the most motivated.

Other sellers will have to be searched out. You'll find them at distress sales, as "for sale by owner" sellers and from Realtors. Many of these property owners are more motivated to sell than you are to buy. That's when bargains are found.

How to Get Others to Bring Properties with Potential to You

Roger and Doris U. are in their 50's. They vacation at least one week a month. They own a large, well-furnished home in the suburbs and over two dozen rental properties. How did they find these properties? Mostly with a small ad in their local newspaper:

READY CASH for your home, paid for or not. Trades welcome. Private party. 555-4567.

Doris recently told me that in one week's time they had *three times* as many properties called in as they could realistically look at. Here's how they handled it:

Beforehand, Roger and Doris talked with bankers and lined up possible loans for worthwhile properties. This way they had a general idea of where they could secure loans *before* they inspected their Properties with Potential.

After placing the ad in their newspaper, Roger and Doris made up a list of questions they wanted to ask and put it by the telephone.

- How many bedrooms? Baths? Garage?
- Are there many rentals in your area?
- What are you asking? Would you consider a lower cash offer?
- Why are you selling?
- May I have your full name and legal description of your property?

How to Get the Answers You Want

To get the most amount of information from callers, Roger and Doris used the "Hot Potato" style of questioning. It's used to get more information than you give, and it goes like this:

CALLER: *Well, that's what my home is like. What will you pay me for it?*

ROGER/DORIS: (Rather than give a specific figure they answer a question with a question:) *How much do you feel it's honestly worth?*

If Roger and Doris think that this is a Property with Potential, they set up an appointment over the phone to see the property. In the meantime, using the legal description and owner's name, they check courthouse records and title companies to gather further information on the property.

HOW TO FIND PROPERTY WITH POTENTIAL

Their inspection of the property includes a check of boundaries, soil type, foundation and condition of any wood, sturdiness of structures and quality of construction, age of wiring and plumbing, condition of garage and other out-buildings, quality of any remodeling or renovation and deciding on the most profitable Selective Improvements they could make to this property. They always make notes.

Finally, they compare the price asked for this unit to other similar units, they estimate what a renter would be willing to pay for this unit, they list any repairs that will have to be made before renting it and they discuss how profitable the unit might or might not be to own. Most important, they don't break the first rule of buying real estate investments:

> *Never fall in love with a property.*
> *Only fall in love with its mathematics.*

Doris is the negotiator and purchaser, and Roger is the handyman. Together they earn a healthy full-time wage with a part-time business: buying, selling and renting Properties with Potential.

Where to Find More Profitable Real Estate Opportunities

By continuing your work as a Rental Expert you can take advantage of distress sales of property and help others while you help yourself.

- TAX DELINQUENT SALES—Check your local courthouse and sheriff's office to find out when regularly scheduled tax sales are held.
- ESTATE SALES—Watch the legal notices in your local newspaper and tell your lawyer to inform you of estate sales.
- DIVORCE SALES—By calling people who have filed for divorce you can often find Properties with Potential.

TRANSFER SALES—Talk with personnel offices and departments of local firms stating that you offer quick, ready cash to buy houses and apartments. They will often pass your name on to company transferees.

FORECLOSURES—Talk with loan officers at your bank, the regional Federal Housing Administration (FHA) and Veterans Administration (VA) about foreclosures and tell them that you're willing to assume mortgages on these properties.

FSBOs Offer a Wealth of PWPs

Another source of Property with Potential is the "for sale by owner" seller found by watching the newspapers and driving through areas with many rentals. The "for sale by owner" sellers—or FSBOs—often have a basic knowledge of real estate sales through buying and selling prior properties, but you can ask them the same questions you would ask the sellers who call in on your ad. Get as much information as you can over the phone, then substantiate the facts before you meet them in person.

You should inspect FSBO property in the same manner as you would call-ins: check the land, then the structure and finally the amenities or extras.

Most important to you is the mathematics. Is the property fairly priced? Would you be able to resell it at a profit in a year? How much would the unit rent for on today's rental market? What type of terms are available?

Another source of good Residential Income properties is your Realtor. A real estate agent is someone licensed to sell real estate, but a Realtor ® is an agent that's a member of the National Association of Real Estate Boards and has pledged to uphold their code of ethics.

Realtors usually charge a 5 to 10 percent brokerage fee, but for that fee you are getting the knowledge and expertise of someone who works full-time at buying and selling real estate in your area. They can usually save you time and money in your real estate transaction. Realtors normally help you set up escrow accounts, start closing

HOW TO FIND PROPERTY WITH POTENTIAL

proceedings, double-check title insurance and understand the often complex world of real estate.

To find a qualified Realtor ask friends and relatives who have purchased Residential Income property to recommend a Realtor. Many Realtors specialize in certain types of properties. They will have more expertise than the Realtor who sells all types of real estate. When you've found the right Realtor to represent you, tell him or her what your plans and goals are. They may be able to show you additional money-making techniques to help you REMAP your future.

Check Properties with Potential for Profitability

You've learned the basics of how real estate profits are made. You've searched for properties that fit your needs and help you complete your financial goals. In fact, you've found a couple of properties that you want to check further for potential profit. Here's how:

Whenever you buy property you want to be assured that you are getting full and legal title and rights to the property, and that no one else has been given the same rights. *Title insurance* companies serve this function. They check the records to see that title to the property is free and clear of encumbrances, then they issue the buyer an insurance policy stating that if the title is not free and clear they will do whatever necessary legally to make it clear at their expense. The seller pays for this policy.

Using CSPs to Check Out a Property

Most title companies also offer another service—usually at little or no cost—that will help you in checking facts given when you inspect property. They offer what is called a *Customer Service Package* which includes a copy of mortgages, liens and maps for any property in your county. They may also include tax figures.

A smart investor becomes friends with at least one local title insurance company officer.

To see how a Customer Service Package—or CSP—works, ask a local title company to build one for a property you are considering for purchase.

To verify the basic facts you've been given by the property owner, look over your CSP and ask these questions:

- Does the seller have full title or rights to sell this property or do others also hold title?
- Does the seller have a mortgage or contract on this property?
- Are there any unpaid tax liens on this property?
- Will the seller be able to clear the title with the cash he'll receive from the sale?
- What did the seller originally pay for this property? How long ago? Under what terms? Can I assume and pay his mortgage or contract? At what interest rate?
- Is this property attached or near an adequate sewer? Does it have a septic tank? How old? In what condition?
- Does this property have adequate water for current use? Future use?
- Who has owned this property during the last ten years? How long? Why did they sell?
- Who built this structure? Who developed the parcel of land?
- Is the unit currently a rental? If so, for how long? What are the monthly rents? How much have they risen during the last two years?
- Are they below, at or above average rents for this unit and location?

How to Verify Profitability

These questions will tell you about the property's past. Here are questions you'll want to consider about your property's future profitability.

- Is this area a slow, medium or fast growth area? Is the trend expected to change in the next few years? Why?
- Does this area need rental units? Why? What services does it offer nearby? Schools? Transportation? Jobs?
- Does this property fit the basic requirements of shelter, location and price for renters?
- How keen is the competition for rentals in this area? Heavy? Moderate? Light? Why?

Your final question on Properties with Potential are designed to help you understand the seller's reason for selling. The answer will give you a clue to the motivation and method of purchasing the property at the most profitable price.

- Ask the seller: "Would you mind telling me why you're selling this property?" Listen intently.
- Then ask: "Are there any other reasons that made you decide to sell?" Then let the seller answer and elaborate before you speak again.

Next, verify those reasons. If the seller says he's selling because he is moving to another city for a new job, verify this with his old and new employer as discreetly as you can. If he says that a divorce is involved, verify that fact and make sure that the seller is authorized to sell the property and can get his spouse's signature in order to release all rights to the property.

Remember, knowledge is potential profit.

How a Buyer Found a Bargain

Russ M. found a property he felt had potential. He ordered a CSP from his title insurance company by giving them the legal description and current ownership of the property. He also asked for tax information.

The Package told him that Frank and Betty L. had purchased the property six years earlier for $26,500 with $2,650 down at 7 percent interest for 30 years. Taxes on the property were $1128 for the year and currently paid in full. The tax assessor gave a value of $43,000 for taxation purposes.

Given a copy of the rent rolls by Mr. and Mrs. L., Russ verified that the current renter had been in the unit two years and that there were only three other renters during the six years they owned it. Phone calls to the previous renters verified facts of length of stay and rents charged. Russ also talked with an old builder in the area who told him about the history of the location and how it was developed. A stop at the city planner's office gave Russ information on what planners felt the area would be like in the coming years and what other rentals were in the area. They also had information on schools and transportation.

The unit rented for $250 a month. After checking the market thoroughly Russ decided that the same unit with minor painting and repairs should rent for about $300 a month.

The seller had told Russ that he was selling because he was moving to the country and wanted to get additional cash to purchase a large parcel of land. Further questioning brought out that the L.'s needed a great deal of cash to pay off delinquent bills.

By checking the facts, history, potential and seller's motivation, Russ was able to satisfy himself of the true value of the property and substantiate the profitable offer he made.

Analyze and Decide about Profitability

Who really sets the price of property?

The *buyer*. The seller only guesses what a buyer would be willing to pay for his property.

How does the intelligent seller arrive at this estimate? There are three different methods used by professional property appraisers. They are:

- Market Analysis method
- Cost method
- Income method

The Property Pricing Sheet on page 53 shows the seller—and the buyer—what other buyers are paying for similar units. The

HOW TO FIND PROPERTY WITH POTENTIAL 51

Pricing Sheet also has a section to estimate value by the Cost method to double-check your Market Analysis.

How to Fill Out Your Property Pricing Sheet

If you've been talking with owners of property about buying and selling, you'll have a pretty good idea of what homes are selling for. You may have heard that a certain house with three bedrooms and two baths in 1100 square feet recently sold for $46,000 on contract terms. A check of courthouse records and assistance from your Realtor will help you substantiate the sale and document the price.

The information in the "For Sale Today" section of your Property Pricing Sheet can be found by calling about similar homes in the newspaper and finding out what the owners are asking for their property, how large the unit is and how they arrived at their price.

The "Sold" section can be filled out with information from courthouse records. The county clerk will have copies of deeds recently recorded and the tax assessors office will have information on square footage, lot size, bedrooms, baths and age of homes. Many title companies will also assist you in compiling comparables.

The "Cost" section will need information from a local builder or your insurance agent on the replacement cost of the unit. You must know what homes of average quality are currently costing to build per square foot, what lot costs are and how much depreciation should be charged against the unit because of age.

How to Analyze Income and Profitability

On page 54 you'll see a sample Income Property Analysis that will show you how to arrive at a fair market value for a Residential Income property based on the income it earns. This unique form can be used to measure profitability on any type of RI property from Single Family Residence to Multi-Family Dwelling.

SECTION 1—*Cash Flow*—In real estate investing, cash flow is the difference between the income from a property and the expenses of operating it. Investors who are looking for a steady income over a long period of time are most interested in purchasing property with a high positive cash flow (more income than expenses). Investors who are more interested in appreciation or growth look for an even cash flow (equal income and expenses). Investors looking for a tax shelter need a negative cash flow (more expenses than income). More on cash flow later.

SECTION 2—*Equity Gain*—This is the amount of principal that will be paid off on the loan by your renters. It is equal to the payment made less the interest paid. It's how much mortgage principal is paid off during a year. It's part of your income from operation.

SECTION 3—*Appreciation*—Inflation causes higher prices and higher values. This higher value is actual income to you collectible when you sell your property. As such you can count it as "paper profits" or an increase in your equity even though you can't spend it until you sell the property or part of the equity.

SECTION 4—*Tax Shelter*—A very important part of investing for those who pay a high percentage of income tax. Tax shelter works like this: if your income from a property is $10,000 a year and the IRS says you can depreciate the property (deduct on paper an amount to cover estimated loss from aging and use) $15,000 a year, you have a $5,000 *tax shelter*. In other words, not only will you not have to pay taxes on the $10,000 income you earned from operating your income property, but you also won't have to pay taxes on $5,000 income from any other source (such as your regular job). Many investors get into real estate investment for this purpose alone.

Finally, to estimate the value you will derive from ownership of a property and to decide what the return on your initial investment is, the final section of my Income Property Analysis has been created.

The Property Pricing Sheet will tell you what an RI property is worth today. The Income Property Analysis will show you what it's worth to you in future benefits. Using these two forms will help you estimate the value of any RI property.

How to Make Even Higher Profits with Residential Income Property

That's not the end of the profits you can earn with RI properties. Not by a long shot. As you'll learn in the coming chapters,

HOW TO FIND PROPERTY WITH POTENTIAL

you can also profit with Creative Purchasing, Accelerated Equity techniques and Productive Marketing.

As you can see, you'll never have to steal a property from an unsuspecting seller in order to make a healthy profit. In fact, you can often pay the seller's full asking price and still make a substantial profit with other investment techniques. There are very few "steals" in real estate investing, but with the knowledge you're developing with the REAL ESTATE MILLIONAIRE PLAN you are beginning to see that there are hundreds—even thousands—of very good and very profitable buys available to you.

Let's learn how to make these good buys even better with the easy-to-learn techniques of Creative Purchasing.

PROPERTY PRICING SHEET

CURRENT OWNER _____ PHONE _____

PROPERTY ADDRESS _____ CITY _____

LEGAL DESCRIPTION _____

LOT SIZE _____ BEDROOMS _____ BATHS ____

FAMILY ROOM ____ GARAGE _____ SQ. FT. ____

YEAR BUILT _____ ASSESSED VALUE ____ TAXES ____

FEATURES _____

IS IT CURRENTLY A RESIDENTIAL INCOME PROPERTY? ____

IF SO, HOW MANY UNITS AND WHAT ARE THE RENTS? ____

COMPARABLES FOR SALE NOW

ADDRESS	LOT SIZE	BEDROOMS	BATH	F/R	SQ.FT.	ASKING PRICE

COMPARABLES RECENTLY SOLD

ADDRESS	LOT SIZE	BEDROOMS	BATH	F/R	SQ.FT.	SALES PRICE

COMPARABLE REPLACEMENT COST

REPLACEMENT COST OF COMPARABLE LOT $ _____

REPLACEMENT COST OF COMPARABLE
  STRUCTURE (Square feet times replacement
  cost per square foot—available from
  builder or insurance agent) $ _____
                          _____

TOTAL REPLACEMENT COST OF
  COMPARABLE RI UNIT $ _____

RECONCILIATION

THE MOST VALUE SHOULD BE GIVEN TO
  THIS RI PROPERTY: $ _____
THE LEAST VALUE SHOULD BE GIVEN TO
  THIS RI PROPERTY: $ _____
PROBABLE MARKET VALUE $ _____

INCOME PROPERTY ANALYSIS

I. CASH FLOW—Income:

    _____ 1-br units @ $ _____ mo. _____
    _____ 2-br units @ $ _____ mo. _____
    _____ 3-br units @ $ _____ mo. _____
  Total Yearly rents (x 12)   _____

CASH FLOW—Expenses:
   Management costs (per month) _____
   Vacancy factor _____
   Taxes and Insurance _____
   Mortgage Payment _____
   Utilities _____
   Total Yearly Expenses (x 12) _____

TOTAL ANNUAL CASH FLOW _____

II. EQUITY GAIN

   Mortgage Payment x 12 _____
   Less Interest Paid _____
   TOTAL EQUITY GAIN _____

III. APPRECIATION

   Purchase Price _____
   Times Appreciation Rate _____
   TOTAL APPRECIATION
   DURING YEAR _____

IV. TAX SHELTER

   Purchase Price _____
   Times Depreciation Rate _____
   TOTAL DEPRECIATION —
   Mortgage Interest Paid _____
   Property Taxes Paid _____
   TOTAL NON-TAXABLE
   EXPENSES _____

TOTAL TAX SHELTER _____
   (Depreciation plus Non-Taxable
     Expenses multiplied by tax rate)

TOTAL CASH FLOW, EQUITY GAIN,
  APPRECIATION AND TAX SHELTER _____

TOTAL LEVERAGE AND RETURN
  ON INVESTMENT _____
  (Total Gain divided by Initial Investment)

3

How to Use Imaginative Financing to Find Start-Up Money for Real Estate Investing

Everybody wants to play the Money Game.

Actually, money is more than just a game—it's an efficient means of placing value on what you do as well as what you want. If you want to buy a new sports car for $10,000 you're not actually giving money for it—you're really exchanging it for $10,000 worth of your time, labor and knowledge. And the person selling you the car really doesn't care whether it took you a day or a year to earn the $10,000. All he wants to know is do you have the cash to exchange with him. Even as you are paying for your car the seller is thinking about all the things he can exchange or buy with the money.

There are only two ways you can gain money and wealth:

(1) You can work hard for it.
(2) It can work hard for you.

You understand how (1) works. This chapter will show you how (2) is used by real estate millionaires.

Money Breeds Money

Jack A. always wanted to breed greyhound dogs. He felt there was a strong market for them. He read all of the books he could on breeding, he took classes on dog breeding and he saved his money to buy his first registered female. He soon mated her with a registered male whose owners would accept the "pick of the litter" in payment. With little cash Jack built his greyhound breeding business into a profitable full-time occupation.

When I first met Jack A. he had decided to use some of these profits to invest in real estate. I found him two rental homes with $4,000 down each. Within three years Jack's equity in these rental homes was over $12,000 each. Jack had used the same principle to purchase and build his rental property as he had with his dog breeding business. Jack knew that a small sum of cash by itself would do little. But combining it with other money—borrowed money—Jack was able to help his money breed more money.

In this chapter you'll learn the basics of breeding money for profit. You'll see how you can use your own small sum of cash to encourage someone to offer you to breed with a larger sum. They get the "pick of the litter"—or interest—and you get the rest.

With this technique you can easily take any small sum of money, make it grow into a larger sum, subdivide it into many small sums, breed them again and continue this process until you've earned the wealth you want.

How to Borrow Profitably

If you were to borrow your neighbor's lawnmower one day to cut your lawn all he would probably ask you to do is to return it within a reasonable time. If you borrowed it to cut other people's lawns for profit he may justly ask you to pay him for the use of his lawnmower. And the rate he asked you to pay would probably depend on how long you plan to borrow it and what the chances are that he'll get it back in one piece.

Borrowing money from a bank is much the same. If you are borrowing funds, the lender assumes that you will profit from its use

HOW TO USE IMAGINATIVE FINANCING

either financially or in comfort and convenience. Your lender will charge you interest based on:

- How long you plan to borrow the money, and
- What the chances are that he'll get his money back.

The longer the term of the loan or the higher the risk, the more money the lender must charge.

To return to my lawnmower analogy, if you can earn five dollars a lawn and cut ten lawns a day you can easily pay the lawnmower's owner ten dollars for the use of the lawnmower and still make a good profit for your labors.

To carry my analogy one step further and show you how *money makes money*, you could rent five lawnmowers at the same rate, pay five young men two dollars each for every lawn they cut and still make a profit of two dollars a lawn for yourself. That's a theoretical $100 a day profit—from using other people's machines and labor.

You're learning how to play the *Money Game*.

How to Use the Power of Leverage for Profits

As you learned in Chapter 1, the Power of Leverage is one of the greatest powers you have in the Money Game. With leverage you can start with little or no actual cash and build your wealth to a quarter million dollars or more in just five short years. Leverage is the power of money to make more money. Leverage is the key to real estate wealth. The best part is that in no other investment opportunity will you find leverage so valuable and so easy to obtain as in Residential Income property investment.

You can see how leverage increases profits. If you expect a profit of 20 percent on a real estate opportunity, you can use the Power of Leverage to borrow five times as much money and make your profit a full 100 percent—actually doubling your money.

Of course, leverage also increases risk. As my analogy would illustrate, the more lawns you cut, the greater the chances that you'll wear out the borrowed lawnmower. Smart entrepreneurs overcome this problem of increased risk with careful planning. With lawnmowers it's a matter of checking the unit out before it's used, making sure there's oil and gas in it, making sure it's tuned-up and taking a few extra minutes to clear obstacles from its path before you start. The point is that careful planning and consideration can reduce the risk that comes with the Power of Leverage.

Also, by lowering risks you not only make your operation more profitable, but you also make it easier to secure a loan from a lender and reuse the Power of Leverage.

How to Get the Loan You Want

Lenders are really not the mean people we imagine them to be. In fact, they need you as much as you need them. Some of them can be down right helpful in showing you how to qualify for a loan with them.

Basically, lenders look at four things in deciding how much of a risk your loan will be:

- YOUR PAST—They want to know what your past history of paying bills has been. Have you borrowed money from others in the past? Did you pay it back? How quickly? How much? Were you able to profit from its use? Do you understand the basics of the Money Game and know how to cut risks?

- YOUR FUTURE—Lenders want to know how you plan to pay back the money you want to borrow. Will you have regular income from the opportunity? How much? Do you have other income that will make the payments in case your opportunity can't?

- THE PROPERTY'S PAST—How old is the unit? Has it been used as an income property before? What rents did it earn? What profit did it make? Can you reasonably expect this trend to continue? Why?

- THE PROPERTY'S FUTURE—Do you plan to make any Selective Improvements to the property? What do you estimate expenses to be? What

HOW TO USE IMAGINATIVE FINANCING

percentage of the gross income will they be? How do you expect to pay back the loan? Will your investment give you a positive cash flow?

If you spend the time to develop the answers to these financial questions for your lender, you'll find him more interested in working with you on your opportunity.

How to Buy Your First Property with Potential Starting with Little or No Cash

The REAL ESTATE MILLIONAIRE PLAN is a proven step-by-step system for finding, negotiating, buying, operating and profiting from the ownership of residential income real estate. Best of all, it offers you the Power of Leverage and the opportunity to build your fortune with little or none of your own capital.

In the coming pages you'll learn—

- 7 Ways to Build Your Breeding Fund
- 4 Places to Borrow Quick Cash
- 3 Successful Methods of Starting with No Cash

And you'll learn how to use these funds to actually rent more money and build your fortune with other people's dollars.

7 Ways to Build Your Breeding Fund

Using Your Savings

The first method of building your Breeding Fund is by getting some or all of it from your savings account. A small investor, though, would never think of withdrawing all of his savings for a single investment. He would be sure to leave enough in his account to cover living expenses for a few months in case of an emergency. A smart investor actually has two funds: "Do Not Disturb" money for a cushion and security, plus a "What the Heck" fund that can be spent on vacations, investments and non-necessities

Sell Real Property

The second way of starting and building your Breeding Fund is to sell real property that you own. David K. found an excellent investment in a three bedroom rental that passed every test. David withdrew $2,000 of his $5,000 savings and sold his two acre recreational parcel in the nearby mountains for enough money to purchase the investment. David realized that his investment would soon pay him back enough to not only buy another parcel in the mountains, but also to give him funds to build on it.

Sell Personal Property

The third method of building your Breeding Fund is to sell personal property such as a car or recreational vehicle you rarely use, major appliances no longer in use, jewelry, furniture or any other valuable excess baggage that you have little use for. They can always be replaced with later profits.

Borrow from Your Assets

Method number four of building your investment fund is to borrow from current assets rather than sell them. In other words, take a mortgage or second mortgage out on real estate you currently own or use personal property as collateral for a loan. This is the best method for investors who want to keep their current assets while increasing their Breeding Fund.

Borrow from Tomorrow

The fifth method calls for taking out a loan with your future pay checks as collateral. More commonly, it's known as a "signature loan."

Clarence R. found the right investment: an older home that had been remodeled by Roger and Doris U. Clarence was renting an apartment when he decided to join the REAL ESTATE MILLIONAIRE PLAN by investing in a home to live in. The sellers offered the home for $24,900 on a real estate contract with $3,000 down. Clarence had no cash on hand so he borrowed from tomor-

HOW TO USE IMAGINATIVE FINANCING 63

row with a signature loan at his credit union for the full $3,000. A year and a half later—after Clarence had made a few Selective Improvements—he sold his home, paid off the credit union and closing costs and still netted over $12,000. Today Clarence is looking for a larger home for himself *plus* a rental for an investment.

Using the Second Mortgage

The sixth way to build your Breeding Fund is with a second mortgage on the property you are planning to buy. A junior or second mortgage is the second loan on the same property. By putting a second mortgage on the property you are buying, you are using the Power of Leverage.

Jim L. found the perfect SFR investment. It was in the right location, in excellent shape and was offered at a reasonable price. Rents were low and vacancies were few. The problem was that the seller wanted a total of 20 percent down on a real estate contract and Jim only had about 10 percent plus closing costs. Jim used the sixth technique for building a Breeding Fund—he found a private lender who would give him the other 10 percent in exchange for a second mortgage on the SFR. Within days Jim was able to close the sale and start making Accelerated Equity on his new RI property.

Loan Yourself

The seventh and final method of building your investment fund is to loan money to yourself. Here's how it works: get a promissory note from your local stationery store and fill it out. Make it a legal document promising to pay yourself the sum of X dollars at the rate of Y dollars a month for Z months. Sign it and have it notarized. Treat this debt as you would any other. Be sure the amount of your payments will fit comfortably into your budget. These monthly funds will come in handy to help you with a negative cash flow, to make Selective Improvements or to pay off a short-term second mortgage or signature loan. Many real estate millionaires have used this method to help build their Breeding Fund and get started on their road to financial success.

Those are the seven best methods of building your real estate Breeding Fund.

4 Places to Borrow Quick Cash

Whether you're building your Breeding Fund or looking for funds to make profitable Selective Improvements, you'll want to remember these next four sources of easy cash.

Conventional Loans

The first place to look for borrowed funds is conventional lending institutions such as banks, savings and loans, credit unions and finance companies. Their credit requirements are sometimes rigid, but each type makes different kinds of loans. S & Ls are the most conservative, followed by banks, credit unions and financial companies. Depending on past credit history and current banking habits, you should be able to find some or all of your funds from one of these institutions.

Instant Cash

Another source of quick, ready cash is credit cards and overdraft accounts. One family who invests in older fixer-uppers has two bank cards—one for personal purchases and the other for building materials, landscaping needs and they've even made a house payment with it. Check overdraft accounts, where you can write checks for more money than you have in your account, are also good sources of quick money for real estate investors. They offer you a source of earnest money for offers on houses as well as an emergency fund. If you don't already have bank cards and overdraft accounts, talk to your banker about signing up for them. They'll improve your credit, too.

Other Investors

The third source of investment funds is other investors. Many people who have made their fortunes prefer to help other entrepreneurs—and help themselves. Rather than put their profits in banks and draw from 5 to 8 percent interest, they rent their money to moneymakers like you and earn 8 to 12 percent. You can find

HOW TO USE IMAGINATIVE FINANCING

these investors through newspaper ads, banking contacts and mortgage brokers.

Associates

The fourth source of funds is made up of the same kind of people—investors who would rather rent their money at a high rate than let a bank or savings and loan hold it at a lower rate. The difference is that these investors are your friends and relatives. Ask around. Many people you know right now would jump at the opportunity to put their savings to work if you can show them how to do it.

But what if you'd rather not borrow against your own assets to start your REAL ESTATE MILLIONAIRE PLAN going? What if you would rather use the Power of Leverage and purchase your first real estate investment with little or no capital of your own? You can do it with one of the following methods.

3 Successful Methods of Starting with No Cash

100 Percent Financing

You can often find 100 percent financing available from lenders who have been forced to repossess property. If you can prove to them that you will be able to repay their loan better than the previous owners, you can often find profitable opportunities in your own community that will allow you to actually take over title in a few days and begin Accelerating Equity with the REAL ESTATE MILLIONAIRE PLAN.

In fact, Haydon J. started his fortune with a bank repossession that needed repair. Not only was Haydon able to take over the property with *no cash*, but the bank was willing to *loan* him $2,000 in cash to fix the unit up so it could be rented profitably and they could get their money out of it.

This technique of 100 percent financing through picking up bank repossessions has been used by hundreds of smart real estate millionaires. You can use it, too. Contact your banker, other community banks, the Federal Housing Administration and Veterans

Administration offices in your area to be kept informed of repossessions that you can take over with 100 percent financing.

Sweeten the Pot

A number of successful investors I know have built their fortunes with no cash by making the seller an offer he just couldn't refuse.

One of them, Tyler D., decided to purchase an older home that was listed at $37,000. It was a three bedroom single-story home in a good rental neighborhood. Tyler knew that the owner owned it free-and-clear, so he made him an offer of $40,000 on the unit with zero dollars down and a payback at 9 percent interest. He told the seller he was willing to sign a Real Estate Contract that would give the seller title to the property until it was paid off. The seller was persuaded.

Two years later, Tyler sold the home for $49,500—a $9,500 profit—and paid the seller off. The property was never actually in Tyler's name, but by sweetening the pot for the seller, Tyler was able to sweeten his own bank account by nearly ten thousand dollars.

Borrow Collateral

Many lenders will lend 100 percent *and more* if you can offer them more than one piece of collateral or security for the loan. And you can borrow other people's collateral just as easily as you'd rent a property. Here's how:

Through investment newsletters, financial publications and newspaper ads you can often find investors who have collateral to rent. They may offer you the use of their $20,00 savings account as collateral for your loan, or $50,000 in equity in a parcel of land, or will offer to use their signature as additional collateral and co-sign for you. Of course, there's a fee for this collateral rental. It may be a flat fee or it may be a few percent interest.

One example involves a longtime friend of mine, Thomas H. Tom had made his fortune many years ago and had bank accounts in nearly every bank in town. One of them—with a balance of $15,000—drew 7 percent interest. This wasn't enough for shrewd

HOW TO USE IMAGINATIVE FINANCING

Tom. He allowed a smart investor to use this account as collateral for a real estate loan. Tom charged the investor 3 percent interest. Tom was then receiving 10 percent interest on his money safely locked in the bank, the investor was able to secure a 100 percent loan to purchase a profitable RI property and the bank had more than enough security to make the loan safely. Everyone was happy.

So don't let the lack of Breeding Funds stop you from taking advantage of the greatest financial opportunity of your lifetime—investing in residential income real estate. Start today with the REAL ESTATE MILLIONAIRE PLAN.

How to Use Conventional Financing to REMAP Your Future

Now that you've built up your Breeding Fund—and know how to start with even no cash—you're ready to buy your first Property with Potential. Let's study the methods you'll use to build your Breeding Fund into over a *quarter million dollars* or more.

Conventional financing is renting money through the conventional lending institutions by using a first mortgage as security.

The largest source of funds to the mortgage market comes from the over 5,400 savings and loan institutions. Normally over 80 percent of their assets are tied up in mortgages.

Another growing segment of the savings industry is the field of mutual savings banks. They operate in only a few states, but the ones that do charter them depend greatly on them for funds to the real estate market.

Traditionally, banks and credit unions are more liberal lenders for short-term loans such as home improvement, the purchase of mobile homes and business capital. Few banks or CUs make loans beyond 15 or 20 years. The real estate investor uses banks and CUs more for Breeding Funds, short-term loans and Selective Improvement loans.

More important to investors are mortgage bankers. A mortgage banker differs from a savings and loan institution in that the bankers don't have depositors' funds on hand to loan, but rather package a loan and sell it to an investor who is looking for a better return than standard bankers give. They are actually loan brokers. They find qualified buyers and match them to an investor who can and will make the loan, then they service the loan and collect their fees. Some mortgage bankers get their money from life insurance companies and pension funds while others work primarily with individual investors. In any case, mortgage bankers are a prime source for real estate investment capital.

How to Secure Your Conventional Financing

Of course, no lender is going to lend a dollar without some type of security. A mortgage is a contract which pledges a specific property as security for the repayment of a debt. The holder of the first mortgage has the first opportunity to legally demand the property and sell it for payment in case of default. The second mortgage holder—or junior mortgage holder—has the second right to proceeds of that sale. The problem with mortgages is that foreclosures often take many months and court costs—and the lenders prefer not to go to that much trouble if they need to get their money back.

Another type of security for a loan—one that overcomes this problem of default—is the trust deed (or deed of trust) that conveys title to the property to a third party or trustee. In this case, the trustee has the power to sell the property if the debtor fails to meet loan conditions within a specified time. Trust deeds keep properties out of the courts and thus are more popular with lenders.

There's a third type of security for loans called land contracts. They'll be covered in detail in a few pages.

Carl B. purchased his first rental unit for $40,000 with a loan from a savings and loan association with $4,000 down plus closing costs. The lender required that Carl sign a trust deed with a local escrow company as the trustor or holder of the deed. The title was still in Carl's name, but in case of default on the loan the title would be transferred by the trustor to the lender.

Using Loan-to-Value Ratios

One term you'll come across often in banking and borrowing is "loan-to-value ratio." The lenders are very concerned about this ratio because it tells them how much equity you have in property and reflects how much you stand to lose if you don't pay the loan off. For example, Carl B. put $4,000 down on his $40,000 rental. In other words, he had a 90 percent loan-to-value ratio. He put up 10 percent and the bank put up 90 percent. They would have felt even more secure with their loan if Carl had put $8,000 or even $16,000 down and given them a loan-to-value ratio of 80 percent or 60 percent respectively.

How Lenders Manipulate Investors for Profit

The availability of money for investors—or what is called "non-owner occupied" mortgages—depends a great deal on what the current money market is like. That is, if a conservative investor feels he can make more in the stock market he'll take more of his savings from his S & L account and put it in the stock market. On a large scale, this changes the amount of money that S & Ls can loan on mortgages. And rather than tell you that they don't have any more money to loan—and risk bad public relations—the S & Ls simply tighten the requirements on borrowing the money they do have. In a free money market lenders are looking desperately for people to borrow from them and will make very easy loans. In a tight money market the lenders often will cut off money to non-owner occupied borrowers or real estate investors first and save their supply of cash for the typical homeowner.

Of course, lenders can also encourage and discourage borrowers through the use of interest rate changes, loan fees and other additional charges.

Financing Secrets Used by Real Estate Millionaires

Here's a method used by real estate millionaires to encourage conventional lenders to loan them money when they need it. Bankers call it "collateralization." It's using a first mortgage on the property being purchased and a first or second mortgage on additional property as collateral for the loan. It gives bankers more security on the loan and they, in turn, offer the investor a better interest rate or a better loan-to-value ratio.

In the example of Carl B., who purchased his non-owner

occupied rental with only 10 percent down, Carl was able to use his own home as part security for the loan by giving the bank a second mortgage on it. With the two mortgages the lender felt safe in making the loan based on such a high "collateralization."

There are also what's known as "insured mortgages." The payment of a mortgage is insured by either a private firm or the federal government. The borrower must pay the insurance fee—normally a fraction of a percent per month—but it allows him to buy a property with a lower loan-to-value ratio and use more leverage in making money with his money.

Insured mortgages are more common than you might think. In fact, all FHA and VA loans as well as most 90 and 95 percent loans made by lenders today are insured loans where the lender is insured for the top 25 percent of value—the riskiest part of the mortgage.

For many years, the Federal Housing Administration (FHA) has been insuring loans for borrowers of primary residences and non-owner occupied mortgages. They charge a flat one-half percent per year fee. By combining capitalism with government, our economic system has not only offered potential homeowners and investors a method of buying homes with low down payments, but the FHA has also created one of the few governmental agencies not dependent on tax dollars.

The Veterans Administration and various state veterans services offer similar insured loans to vets, the difference being that vets don't pay the insurance fee—the government does. Up to 100 percent mortgages are available.

The FHA offers loans for non-owner occupied homes and income property with an additional 15 percent down. The VA does not. But both FHA and VA loans are at interest rates lower than conventional loans and they are assumable under certain conditions.

Why Sellers Pay Points on FHA and VA Loans

The reason why interest rates on FHA and VA loans are lower than conventional loans is because the seller has made up the difference by paying what is called "points" or prepaid interest. While FHA and VA interest rates don't change as often as conventional rates, the slack is taken up by the fluctuating "points" charged to the seller on a sale by this method. You'll see FHA and VA loans in action in your Wealth Years.

Conventional mortgage lenders differ in their purpose, method, operation and cost of loans. Most home mortgages are made through conventional lenders, but the investor has another alternative that offers opportunity and creativity: Imaginative Financing.

How to Build Your Fortune with Imaginative Financing

The drawback of conventional financing is that the institutions who are lenders—savings and loans, banks, mortgage companies, credit unions—are conservative by nature. After all, they're lending OPM: Other People's Money. Lenders who offer their own money are usually not as conservative and will often lend money based on facts that cannot be read on a loan application.

In many cases, interest rates are higher for Imaginative Financing because of higher risk, but they can also be lower because of lower administration costs.

There are basically four types of Imaginative Financing: contracts, wrap-around seconds, assumptions and sweat equity. Together they offer dozens of variations and methods of using the Power of Leverage to build your fortune with the REAL ESTATE MILLIONAIRE PLAN.

A contract—or real estate contract—serves the same purpose as a mortgage but in a different way. Rather than getting your loan at a bank, letting the bank pay the seller his cash and having you make the payments to the bank, a real estate contract has you paying the seller directly. He is actually financing his own property. The advantage to the seller is that rather than getting a lump sum of cash and putting it back in the bank at the going interest rate, he can charge you something near the mortgage rate—2 or 3 percent higher than the deposit rate—and earn more money on his money.

The advantage to you as a buyer is that the seller is often more lenient with credit since he continues to hold title under contract until you pay the contract off. For this and other reasons, a contract often requires less down than a non-owner occupied conventional loan.

Pay-off Methods

You can make a contract pay-off in two different ways:

- Amortizing
- Balloon

An amortizing contract is one that has equal monthly payments for a specific amount of time, at which the contract is completely paid off. Nearly all conventional loans are amortizing.

A balloon contract is different. Rather than being paid off in 15, 20 or 30 years some contract sellers want their money in a few years. Their answer is to hold a contract with an "early cash-out" or balloon payment in a few years.

Remember Clarence R.? He purchased his first investment property on a real estate contract with $3,000 borrowed from a credit union. His contract had a two year cash-out. In other words, at the end of two years Clarence was to give the sellers a lump sum payment for the balance of the contract. How could he do this? By either selling the property or refinancing it based on its higher appreciated value in two years.

A typical balloon payment contract would suggest 10 to 20 percent down payment, payments of about 1 percent of the balance per month, with a three, five or ten year cash-out.

How Second Mortgages Are Used by the Real Estate Pros

Previously we discussed second mortgages. Many investors have sold property where the purchaser found an 80 percent conventional loan, offered 10 percent down and carried a 10 percent second mortgage on the property. Some sellers prefer a variation of this method called a "Wrap-Around." A wrap-around is offered by the seller and, in the example above, the seller would accept your 10 percent down and have you make payment on the balance directly to him. He would charge you the going rate of interest for the 90 percent loan amount, but would be able to pay the underlying mortgage off at a lower interest rate. If his underlying mortgage was for about 50 percent of the purchase price, he would get full interest for 40 percent and part interest on the 50 percent.

Many sellers consider wrap-arounds when it would be difficult for the purchaser to finance the property through conventional lenders because of a high prepayment penalty to the seller or a tight money market.

Another method of using Imaginative Financing is assuming an underlying loan. In other words, if you are purchasing an RI property from someone who already has a mortgage on it, you can often assume and pay off the mortgage for him. If there is a wide gap between the purchase price and the assumable loan, consider asking the seller to take a second mortgage for part of the difference.

Why Smart Investors Use Assumptions

The advantage to assuming a loan rather than getting a new one are many:

- The underlying mortgage may be at a lower interest rate allowing you to pay less for the money you borrow.
- When you assume someone elses loan, you are usually not subjected to the close scrutiny by their loan department that they give conventional new loans.
- Closing costs are lower on assumptions. Most conventional loans require a 1 to 3 percent loan fee. Assumptions usually require a small assumption fee of $100 to $500. Rarely more.

In Chapter 4 you'll learn how to write a profitable offer based on assuming the underlying mortgage.

The final method of using Imaginative Financing is called "sweat equity," and it works like this:

Dave and Peggy R. decided to buy an apartment complex in a high growth area. After doing an analysis of the property, they decided that it was below market value but that it needed new roofing, a complete paint job inside and out and minor plumbing repairs—things that Dave and Peggy decided would make profitable Selective Improvements.

The sellers were an older couple who wanted to retire.

The proposition that Dave and Peggy made to the sellers was this: the asking price—below market value—was $180,000. The buyers aggeed to pay the full market price of $200,000 for the property by signing a note for $170,000 and getting a "sweat equity" credit toward the down payment of $30,000. The note was amortized for ten years offering the sellers $2,153.78 a month on which to retire.

The buyers were able to purchase the property with *no cash down* by making the repairs needed to bring it up to market value.

As you can see, there are dozens of ways of reaching your own financial goal when you understand and use the principles of *multiplying real estate profits* with Imaginative Financing.

4

How to Use Creative Purchasing to Negotiate Profitable Real Estate Transactions

Donna S. wanted to beat the interest the banks were offering her. She had $5,000 in cash to invest and wanted to buy her first rental home. With Creative Purchasing I helped her buy a brand new home directly from the builder. The offer we made was this:

> Full price: $36,950. Purchaser agrees to assume and pay builder's mortgage of $30,000. Purchaser shall pay $5,000 down and sign a note and second mortgage for $1,950 at $25 a month with balance due within two years of closing. Seller shall pay normal buyer's closing costs.

The offer was accepted and Donna had her first profitable RI property. Through Selective Improvements and other Accelerated Equity techniques, Donna's SFR increased in value by $5,000 the first year. She actually *doubled* her money in 12 months.

And she beat the bank.

Creative Purchasing is learning how to buy the most profitable properties for the lowest price on the easiest terms. It's minimizing normal risks by knowing how to negotiate a profitable deal. Creative Purchasing is one of the most important steps in the REAL ESTATE MILLIONAIRE PLAN.

How to Take the Wind Out of Real Estate Risk

Everything you do—from getting up in the morning to driving home from work—involves a certain amount of risk. Risk is exposure to the chance of loss or injury. If you cross the street, you are running the risk of being hit by a car. If you climb a ladder, you are running the risk of falling. Even if you put your money in a bank, you are running the risk of losing it. Anytime you say that things will be the same tomorrow as they are today, you are running the risk of being wrong.

Of course, you minimize risks by learning what you can about the risks involved *before* you run into them. Then you take action to cut your risks to a minimum. As you cross the street, you walk in the crosswalk and watch around you in preparation for action if the risk of getting hit suddenly becomes too great.

All real estate opportunities are based on a forecast of the future. Your profits are in the future—and so are the risks of loss. When you pay a certain price for a parcel of real estate, what you are actually paying for is the present worth of future benefits. You are paying or promising to pay X number of dollars today in order to receive Y number of dollars or benefits tomorrow and in the future.

Crossroad Risks

Further, there are *Crossroad Risks* involved. If your road to opportunity has a 90 percent chance of taking you where you want to go and you come to a crossroad—or decision point—you must

HOW TO USE CREATIVE PURCHASING

make a decision involving risk. If there's an 80 percent chance that the road to the right is the correct one and you take it, your risk factor is not now 80 percent, but 90 percent *times* 80 percent or 72 percent risk factor. And every crossroad you come to demands another decision and another increase in risk.

The solution to the problem of risk is simple—gather all available information on each opportunity and eliminate:

- Opportunities that will not take you to your goal.
- Opportunities that will not take you to your goal in the most direct path.

To apply this solution to the problem of deciding among many real estate investment opportunities, you must first *gather* all of the information you can on each opportunity you are considering. You must spread out each opportunity so you can view the entire group. And you must have your goals clearly in mind.

Then *study* each opportunity with this question: how many dollars will this opportunity offer me for the number of dollars I offer to it? In other words, what is my return per dollar invested? In the case of Donna S., her return was *100 percent* in the first year.

The third step is to *recheck* the opportunities for factual data. Review the information you have on your Income Analysis Sheets. Which opportunity offers the best cash flow? Appreciation? Leverage? Lowest risk? Net return?

Using the Plus and Minus Sheet

Finally, choose two or three of the best opportunities to study further with my PLUS AND MINUS SHEET. A PLUS AND MINUS SHEET makes you list the advantages and disadvantages to an opportunity. It helps you make the best decision because it requires that you consider all aspects of the investment opportunity before you decide.

Donna's PLUS AND MINUS SHEET on the property she eventually purchased looked like this:

PLUS AND MINUS SHEET

PLUS	MINUS
Opportunity to increase rate of return over that offered by bank.	Risk of losing investment due to change in market conditions.
Terms are easy to meet with rents charged. Will pay itself off.	Risk that property won't stay rented and I'll have to make payments.
New home requires little or no maintenance.	Will have to interview many people to find suitable renters.
Can use accelerated depreciation.	
Well-built home with one year contractor's waranty.	
Some Selective Improvements can be made to further increase home's value.	

How to Overcome the Minuses

Donna was able to overcome many of the MINUSES. She studied the local real estate market and realized that the chance of losing her original $5,000 investment was almost nonexistent. To overcome the MINUS of making a payment, Donna lowered the rental just a few dollars a month to ensure that the tenant wouldn't be "rent shopping." Finally, I showed Donna a method of screening renters that I'll show you in a later chapter. It cut down the hassles and put the best renters in the unit within days.

Then it was time to decide. Donna had looked at three different Residential Income opportunities. Two were preowned homes and one was the new home. One of the preowned homes was outside of a good rental area and on the fringe of a declining neighborhood. For this and other reasons Donna ruled this one out. The other preowned home was a well-built home in a good rental neighborhood near schools and shopping—but it required nearly $10,000 down payment plus another $2,000 or more to bring it back to good condition. One of Donna's investment goals was to have homes that required little care or maintenance. The new

HOW TO USE CREATIVE PURCHASING

home best suited all of her requirements—including leverage—and she decided to make an offer.

As you saw in the opening of this chapter, Donna made a full price offer. Why? Because in doing so she was able to change the terms of the offer to include a short-term second mortgage to cover the $1,950 difference between what she had and the seller's price. She also saved cash by having the seller pay her closing costs.

Today Donna's investment is still rented and still earning her money. One renter asked to put up a fence. Donna suggested that if they would agree to stay one year she would purchase the materials. The renter agreed to stay and put the fence up. Donna not only got a very profitable and very permanent renter, but she also earned a Selective Improvement that added value to her property.

How to Make Your Offer on Property with Potential

In most states, an offer to purchase a property—often called a Purchase and Sale Agreement—has the same requirements. It must be in writing and contain:

- Legal description of the property
- Price and terms
- Escrow instructions
- Earnest money
- Signatures of purchaser and seller

Your attorney can draw this agreement up, your Realtor can prepare and present the offer or you can buy Purchase and Sale Agreement forms at large stationery stores and some title companies. The forms are very general in nature to cover a variety of transactions.

The Importance of Legal Descriptions

The description of the property you are making an offer on must be more than just "1328 NE Filmore Street." It must be a legal description that will identify both the location and the boundaries. There are three types of legal descriptions in general use:

GOVERNMENT SURVEY	NE¼ of the N½ of Section 27, Township 2 North, Range 3 East of the Willamette Meridian
RECORDED MAPS	Lot 2, Evergreen Estates-2
METES AND BOUNDS	Thence West 80 rods, thence South 20 rods, thence East 80 rods, thence North 20 rods to the point of beginning.

To make an offer of fair market value and to take clear title you will want to have a complete, accurate and legal description of the property you are buying. The seller will purchase a title insurance policy in your favor that insures he is able to give title to this property. The policy also offers to insure against boundary disputes, but you must first be satisfied that boundaries represented by the seller are the actual boundaries of the property.

Price and Terms

If you've followed the REAL ESTATE MILLIONAIRE PLAN, you know exactly what the property you've decided on is worth on today's market—and in future benefits to you. The price you offer is very important, but I'll pass along something a multi-millionaire real estate investor told me:

> *The terms of a purchase are twice as important as the price.*

Since then I've learned that this may be a *conservative* estimate—that the terms may be *more than twice* as important. In any case, they're the most important part of your offer and I'll show you how to write up the best terms in just a moment. Let's finish up on the parts of a Purchase and Sale Agreement.

Escrow Instructions

Next, your Agreement will serve as instructions to the escrow company or bank escrow department where you close your transaction. Most Purchase and Sale Agreements available from attorneys

HOW TO USE CREATIVE PURCHASING

or forms available from stationers will cover escrow instructions, but check to make sure that the closing date, financing methods and distribution of funds are covered to your satisfaction. An escrow is nothing more than a disinterested third party who agrees to exchange the necessary cash and papers for the buyer and seller and see that the proper documents get recorded.

Getting Your Earnest Money

Finally, a Purchase and Sale Agreement requires some type of deposit by the buyer to make it legal and ensure that he will actually buy the property at closing. This is called "earnest money" and can be in many forms. It can either be cash, a promissory note or an offer of equity. The earnest money deposit usually ranges from one-half to two percent of the total purchase price—$200 to $800 on a $40,000 property. The earnest money can also be in the form of a promissory note, or promise to pay at a later date. Many buyers give earnest money in the form of a "note due on acceptance of the offer" and put their earnest money on deposit with the escrow company only after the offer has been accepted by the seller. The offer of equity earnest money is more unusual. One such Agreement I saw offered a pick-up truck as the earnest deposit. If the buyer didn't buy as he promised, the seller would be driving a new pick-up truck.

Real estate can be fun. All that's needed is your signature as the buyer and the seller's signature to make your Purchase and Sale Agreement a legally binding contract. As promised, we'll go over how to write the best terms, then I'll show you how to present your offer to the seller for his signature.

How to Write Your Own Terms

Again, terms are the most important part of any offer. They often make the difference between a good deal and a great one. Smart investors don't offer full cash as the purchase price. They use the Power of Leverage and offer terms. In deciding what terms you will offer, consider your:

- Available funds
- Desired leverage

- Methods of financing
- Needs of the seller

To illustrate the different types of terms you can offer I'll use actual examples of terms offered on successful Purchase and Sale Agreements. You, your attorney or your Realtor can modify them as you need to fit your situation or local laws.

Every Purchase and Sale Agreement has wording something like this:

TOTAL PURCHASE PRICE IS _____ DOLLARS, PAYABLE AS FOLLOWS:

This is where the terms are outlined.

CONVENTIONAL FHA/VA FINANCING	PURCHASER AGREES TO PAY ENTIRE PURCHASE PRICE BY PAYING $ _____ DOWN, INCLUDING EARNEST MONEY, AND BALANCE BY PROCEEDS OF AN (FHA, VA, 80%, 90% CONVENTIONAL) MORTGAGE, WHICH HE AGREES TO SECURE IMMEDIATELY.
ASSUME EXISTING MORTGAGE OR CONTRACT (Make sure the mortgage or contract is, in fact, assumable)	PURCHASER AGREES TO PAY $ _____ DOWN, INCLUDING EARNEST MONEY, TO A NOW EXISTING (MORTGAGE or REAL ESTATE CONTRACT) IN THE APPROXIMATE CURRENT BALANCE OF $ _____, ON WHICH THE MONTHLY PAYMENTS ARE APPROXIMATELY $ _____. PURCHASER AGREES TO ASSUME AND PAY SAID (MORTGAGE or CONTRACT) ACCORDING TO ITS OWN TERMS AND CONDITIONS.
SELLER TAKES A SECOND MORTGAGE BACK	Add to above terms: BALANCE OF PURCHASE PRICE IN THE AMOUNT OF $ _____ SHALL BE IN THE FORM

HOW TO USE CREATIVE PURCHASING

	OF A NOTE SECURED BY A SECOND (MORTGAGE or TRUST DEED) ON THE PROPERTY, TO BE EXECUTED BY THE PURCHASER IN FAVOR OF THE SELLER AND PAYABLE AT $ _____ PER MONTH, OR MORE, INCLUDING INTEREST AT _____ % PER ANNUM.
REAL ESTATE CONTRACT	PURCHASER WILL PAY $ _____ DOWN, INCLUDING EARNEST MONEY, AND AGREES TO SIGN A REAL ESTATE CONTRACT FOR THE BALANCE OF $ _____. TOTAL MONTHLY PAYMENTS SHALL BE $ _____ OR MORE, AND SHALL INCLUDE INTEREST AT THE RATE OF _____ % PER ANNUM COMPUTED ON THE DIMINISHING PRINCIPAL BALANCE. PURCHASER SHALL PAY ALL TAXES AND INSURANCE WHEN DUE.

These are suggested wordings, but the content is very important. Two of the most important words in the terms are "or more." These two words allow the purchaser to pay the mortgage or contract off early if he desires. Without them he cannot.

You, as the buyer, may want to put additional conditions or contingencies on your offer. Here are some that are used in successful Purchase and Sale Agreements:

To get cash with a second mortgage on other property.	THIS OFFER IS SUBJECT TO PURCHASER SECURING A SECOND MORTGAGE ON PROPERTY LOCATED AT _____ WITHIN _____ DAYS OF THE ACCEPTANCE OF THIS OFFER.

If there is a prior offer that may not go through.	THIS OFFER IS SUBJECT TO PRIOR PURCHASE AND SALE AGREEMENT DATED _____. PURCHASER AGREES TO REMAIN IN BACK-UP POSITION UNTIL _____.
Inspection by relative, pest inspector or contractor.	THIS OFFER IS SUBJECT TO SATISFACTORY INSPECTION OF PROPERTY BY _____ WITHIN _____ DAYS OF THIS AGREEMENT.
Purchaser needs to sell other property first.	THIS OFFER IS SUBJECT TO PURCHASER SELLING PROPERTY LOCATED AT _____ WITHIN _____ DAYS OF THIS AGREEMENT.
Seller promises to make repairs.	THIS OFFER IS SUBJECT TO SELLER MAKING THE FOLLOWING REPAIRS PRIOR TO CLOSING . . .
Seller guarantees rent rolls are correct.	SELLER WARRANTS THE ACCURACY OF THE ATTACHED AND SIGNED STATEMENT OF RENTAL INCOME AND EXPENSES.

You'll be introduced to more clauses and techniques as I guide you through each of the five Wealth Stages. For now these clauses and conditions will give you an idea of how an offer is made on a property to ensure a profit before the property is actually closed.

How to Present Your Offer to the Seller

It's time.
You've worked with your attorney, Realtor, partner or by your-

HOW TO USE CREATIVE PURCHASING

self to bring the offer and terms to the best situation for you while not tying the seller's hands. It's time to present your offer to the seller.

Before you do, reread the entire Purchase and Sale Agreement for clarity. Make sure that the wording and your intent are clear and that what you are asking for is not contradictory.

Then take a moment to consider and understand the seller. Why is he or she selling the property? What do they expect to get out of selling the property? Cash? How much? What will they use the funds for? Do they want a contract offering them long-term income? How much?

Finally, prepare yourself with optimism. Realize that this opportunity is not a life-and-death situation, but that you stand to make a healthy profit if you can purchase this property. Estimate your profit in advance and keep this general figure in mind. Know your limits. If there is need for long negotiations, you must know what you can offer and still profit.

You're presenting your offer to the seller. He's not the enemy, he's a potential friend. As you greet him, smile and show him that you're not his enemy either. Allow him to relax his guard. Sit down at a dining room or conference table and keep your offer in a folder while you exchange small talk about common things. If you've learned that he's from your home state, or likes the same football team you do, or has the same hobbies, talk about them. Get to know the seller and help him relax with you.

As you present your offer don't be apologetic. You have probably studied the property's value more than he has. Take the offer out and explain it—don't read it—to him. If other signatures, such as a wife's or partner's, are needed to accept the deal, make sure they are also present to hear your offer.

Start by telling the seller about the positive things and the small concessions that he has won. Then move to a general outline of the terms. Finally, move to the actual price. Of course, if the price is full and the terms are cut, start with the price and then move to the terms. By that time the seller will often expect the worst and you can often psyche him up for a lower offer than you made—and please him with a better one.

Presenting an Offer to Ensure Acceptance

Here's how I presented the offer for Donna S. when she purchased her first rental home outlined at the start of this chapter.

"Gentlemen, I have some very good news for you. I have an offer on your home at 7316 NE 145th Court that I sincerely feel will be a good transaction for both you and my client, Donna S.

"First, let me tell you a little about Donna. She's a hard working young woman who has spent the last 9 years building a career in management. Her current income is more than sufficient to handle the payments on this property if it were vacant and not bringing in rents. I think she's someone you'd be pleased to have as a purchaser.

"The good thing about her offer to you gentlemen is that the whole transaction can close and you can have your money within just a couple of weeks, which I'm sure is important to you. And, best of all, her offer is for the full price you're asking for the property.

"The terms are also close to what you requested. She has agreed to assume and pay your mortgage—plus give you $5,000 in cash on closing. All she's asking for is that you carry a small second mortgage for the balance of $1,950 for just two years. I'm sure you can live with that."

How to Negotiate a Profitable Deal

Once the offer has been presented, the seller has three choices:

- Accept the entire offer
- Completely reject the offer
- Accept some of the terms and reject others

Many transactions will end with the seller wanting to accept some of the terms offered, but wanting to change other terms. At that time a good negotiator will remind him:

"Mr. Seller, what we have here is a bona fide offer from a qualified purchaser. I'm sure that you understand that if you change anything in this offer—even change the price or terms five dollars—the purchaser doesn't have to accept it and you've lost a valuable offer. If, on the other hand, you can live with the terms of this offer, all you have to do is put your approval on the bottom of this Agreement (place Agreement and pen in front of the seller) and your property is sold and the money is yours."

You can use the same technique for presenting your own offer by saying that you have spent a considerable amount of time and energy deciding on what this property would be worth *to you* and that you have made the best offer you can. Any counter offer made by the seller would have to be in writing, be considered at length and might be rejected. Hint that you are considering other investment properties at the same time.

Of course, from a negotiation standpoint, it's better to have your offer presented by a Realtor, your attorney or other competent person. It's usually easier for a third party to hold out for you.

How to Successfully Handle an Owner's Counter Offer

If your sellers insist on changing some terms of your offer—or reject your offer completely—do these things:

- Get approval on minor points
- Find similarities between the buyer's and seller's needs
- Minimize differences
- Use the See-Saw technique of negotiation

For example, if the difference between you and the seller is price, switch the subject to things you agree on and get the seller to commit his approval.

"Okay, Mr. Seller, we seem to be $5,000 apart on the price . . . but we both agree that you are looking for a real estate contract that will pay you an income for at least five years, am I right?"

The See-Saw Negotiating Techniques

The See-Saw technique of negotiating is a trading of terms. You give something the seller wants—and you also get something you want. To carry the example further:

"Mr. Seller, I think I know of a way that you can get your higher price. I will agree to pay you 10 percent interest rather than the 9 percent I have offered you. My calculations tell me that over the 20 year term of this loan, the increase in interest rates will give you an extra $6,266.40 in income. *In exchange*, I will make my own down payment $4,000 instead of $5,000. This seems fair, doesn't it?"

You've offered to *exchange* one purchaser's concession for a seller's concession. You haven't given away anything. In fact, by changing your monthly payments just a few dollars you've been able to increase your leverage position. When sellers balk at terms or price, rather than give away profit points, negotiate and trade concessions—that's the See-Saw technique.

The seller has signed the deal. Both the buyer and seller have agreed on price and terms of the sale. You've reduced your negotiations and agreement to writing so that the lending institution or escrow company can close the transaction for you. Following are some profitable techniques on closing.

How to Close Your Transaction Profitably

There are actually three different closings to a sale:

- *Agreement Closing*—when buyer and seller agree on price and terms and sign the Purchase and Sale Agreement.
- *Legal Closing*—when all documents needed to transfer title have been signed and recorded.
- *Financial Closing*—when the funds paid by the buyer are given to the seller.

Once you've completed your Agreement Closing and have the seller's signature on your Purchase and Sale Agreement, you can start the Legal Closing by taking the Agreement and any other needed documents to the lending institution or escrow company. They will draw up the necessary papers for the Legal and eventual Financial Closings.

Closing costs on a transaction vary greatly with the type of financing, the excise tax on the sale, loan fees, assumption fees and other variables. Your closing officer will be able to estimate the closing costs for both the buyer and seller when you give him or her your transaction papers.

As far as closing costs are concerned, the seller is usually responsible for:

- Drawing documents in favor of the purchaser;
- Documentary stamps on the deed;
- Notary fee on any instruments in favor of the purchaser;
- Title insurance policy fee (in most areas);
- Broker's commission (if any).

And the purchaser is usually responsible for:

- Drawing documents in favor of the seller or, if financing is involved, in favor of the lender;
- Recording fee for deed in favor of himself and deed of trust in favor of the lender;
- Notary fee on any instruments in favor of the seller or lender.

Also included in the closing costs are Prorations. The closing officer will divide the charges and credits due the buyer and seller for taxes, insurance and rents, and give a credit or debit to the proper party on their closing or settlement sheet.

How to Close in Escrow

The day soon comes when the escrow officer of your bank, title company or escrow company calls to set an appointment for you and the seller to separately sign the closing papers. If you have a broker or attorney handling your transaction, ask him to look over the closing papers before you come in to sign them.

As soon as you know when the closing date is, you should pull all of your papers on the purchase—Purchase and Sale Agreement, any counter offers, your preliminary title insurance policy and your Income Analysis Sheet—and review the points of the transaction.

—How will you take title? Individual, partnership or corporation?
—Are their rents to be prorated?
—Is the legal description correct?
—Have you verified the income from this property, if any?
—Have you and the seller removed all of the conditions from the agreement? Financing? Inspection?

In most cases you and the seller will sign the closing papers at different times on the same day. If you are required to bring additional cash at closing, make sure it is a certified or cashiers check. A personal check can often hold up the closing process.

After the papers are signed, the closing officer will record the deed, mortgage and other papers needed at the courthouse. Then comes the third and final closing: the Financial Closing. The seller gets his funds and you are now the proud owner of your first Residential Income property.

Now you can learn how to Accelerate Equity for quick profits.

5

How to Accelerate Equities for Higher Real Estate Profits

The REAL ESTATE MILLIONAIRE PLAN,

PWP × IF + CP × AE + PM = SP

shows you that profits are *multiplied* by *Accelerated Equity*. This chapter will show you exactly how profits are made with RI properties and how you can multiply your profits with Accelerated Equity techniques.

First, let's look at the one factor that makes RI properties more profitable than any other type: the renter. Just what is a renter? It's a person or persons who pay the owner of a property for the *use* of that property. The renter is, by nature, temporary. He trades his dollars for the right to use a property for his own comforts. He is looking for three basic things:

- Location
- Features
- Cost

What is a *profitable* renter? One who offers you:

- A fair return on your investment dollar
- Prompt and full payment of rents due
- Minimal expenses and maintenance costs
- No headaches

As you study why people rent SFRs and MFDs and how to make them profitable, you'll find that renters can be grouped into types:

- Young families starting out
- Retirees looking for inexpensive housing
- Adult singles
- Young singles
- Home buyers waiting for their homes to be built
- Transfers to area jobs
- Perennial renters

Finding Profitable Renters

The next question is: how do you find profitable renters?

You *advertise* for them. You place an ad in one or more local newspapers, put a sign on the property and tell local real estate agents about the rental. Remembering what renters are looking for, your ad will include:

- Location (tell them what neighborhood, community or city it's located in).
- Features (how many bedrooms, baths, size of garage, condition, appliances)
- Cost (monthly rents and deposits required)

Then identify yourself with a telephone number to call. A good ad may read something like this:

> SIFTON AREA 3 bedroom home with stove, refrigerator and fireplace. $300 a month plus deposit. Call 555-4534.

HOW TO ACCELERATE EQUITIES

As potential renters call, have a list of questions by your phone that you will want to ask them. To find profitable renters, you must be choosey and set your minimum requirements that renters must meet. I developed this TENANTS QUALIFYING SHEET for one of my clients:

TENANTS QUALIFYING SHEET

Potential tenants must prove:

- At least a 3½-to-1 gross salary to rent ratio. (For his $300 a month SFR I suggested that renters prove at least $1,000 a month gross salary.)

- Steady employment. (1 year or more in the same field, but not necessarily at the same firm.)

- Credit. (Renters fill out credit applications and must have a fairly clean credit report and good banking references.)

- References from at least two landlords. (One of the most important qualifying questions.)

- Automobile. (Their vehicle must be clean, but not necessarily newer.)

- No large indoor pets. (Medium or smaller domestic pets only. Pet deposit or fee should be charged.)

- No singles or roommates. (For SFRs—a house rental is for families. Renting to roommates is best left to apartment owners.)

- No more than two persons per bedroom. (A three bedroom home should have no more than six people living in it. Overcrowding causes excessive wear on your home.)

- Refrigerator. (Again, home renters should

be more stable. If they don't own a refrigerator they are more transient and should consider renting an apartment.)
- Pay first, last and deposit. (Require the first and last month's rent *in advance* of moving in along with a refundable damage deposit.)

These ten requirements for SFR home renters can be liberalized to suit your MFD or apartment renters, keeping in mind that people who can afford to rent a home are generally higher paid and more stable. Apartments have higher turnovers, but also return more rent per dollar invested than do SFRs. Higher profits mean higher risks.

No matter what you're renting, have your renters sign a rental agreement. You can get them from local stationery stores or area rental owner councils. Most rental agreements are little better than a handshake as far as the law is concerned, but renters will respect their responsibilities and your rules more if they feel you have an agreement in writing.

How to Initiate Renters to Your Rules

Whether you're renting a house, a duplex or an apartment, you should have a list of rules and guidelines that you can have your tenants sign and keep for future reference. Basically, your Renter's Rules should outline what you are offering and what you expect from them in return. A sample reads like this:

RENTERS RULES

This agreement between <u>Bill and Donna Ramos</u> as tenants and <u>Mike and Nadine Richards</u> as owners of <u>2537 NE Las Gatos Way, Eureka, CA</u> for the month-to-month rent of said property until such time as the tenant or owner gives the other at least 20 days notice in writing to vacate the property. Monthly rent shall be $300 per month paid on the <u>1st</u> of each month. The rent shall be <u>$325</u> if paid after the <u>10th</u> of that month. In

HOW TO ACCELERATE EQUITIES

exchange for this payment the named tenants have the rights to use the property as their residence without interference from the owner provided they accept these obligations:

- The tenants maintain the home as their own and don't subject it to undue wear and tear.
- The tenants maintain the lawn and yard with pride.
- The tenants notify the owner immediately of any emergency that could cause damage to the home.
- The tenants assist the owner with any minor repairs needed to the home such as leaky faucets, broken windows, etc.
- The tenants have no pets other than those cleared in advance with the owner, and care for such pets so they don't cause damage to the property. The owner acknowledges approval of the following tennant's pet(s): <u>1 small male poodle dog named "Charlie."</u>
- In the event of undue damage to the property, the owner shall have the option of giving the tenants five (5) days written notice to vacate and shall have repairs needed charged against the damage deposit for the tenants. Normal home maintenance will not be included in repair charges.

We agree to abide by these rules.

_____   _____
Tenant   Owner

_____   _____
Tenant   Owner

_____   _____
Date   Date

As you can see, the suggested Rental Rules is not a legal document, but is a strong agreement because it shows the intent of the owner and the tenant. Some of the terms and phrases such as "undue wear and tear" are subject to interpretation, but complete legal language to cover all the possibilities may scare tenants off from the real intent of the agreement: to notify the tenant of his rights and obligations in an understandable manner.

How to Keep Rentals Profitable

To make a profit, your income must be more than your expenses. Pretty basic. But how can you keep income up while you keep vacancies down—and services up while you minimize expenses? With a careful analysis of the necessary and the unnecessary.

Let's take a look at income. Your income from a rental unit is, of course, rents. If you price them too high your renters will move to less expensive, yet comparable units. If you price them too low your renters will stay, but your units will be less profitable than they could be. The rents you set on your units are very important.

As promised, there are three ways of setting your rents profitably:

- Income Method
- Market Data Method
- Cost Method

The Income Method

The first is the INCOME METHOD. How much income do you expect your investment to return to you? Ten percent a year? Twelve percent? This percentage of return is your *capitalization rate*. This is the amount of return you expect each year from your total investment.

Keep in mind that this return is on the full value of your property and not just your investment. A capitalization rate of 10 percent per year on an investment where you have used 10 percent leverage will theoretically give you a 100 percent return each year on your original investment.

Here's an example of how to set rents using the Income Method: you have a 12-unit apartment complex valued at

HOW TO ACCELERATE EQUITIES

$240,000. If your capitalization rate is 10 percent, you expect an income of $24,000 a year from the operation of this project. This is $2,000 per unit per year or $167 per unit per month. This return will come from many sources: rents, appreciation, depreciation tax shelter, income tax savings. On these units you should have an after-expenses income of $167 a unit each month. Add your normal expenses to this figure and you have an approximate rental charge that will be profitable.

The Market Data Method

The MARKET DATA METHOD will then tell you if renters are actually willing to pay that amount of rent for your units. The Market Data Method involves comparing your units with what other rental owners are successfully charging. Of course, there are probably no exact duplicates of your rental unit and location, but you can use a Comparison Scale to help you. Here's an example:

Your unit is a three bedroom, one bath home with 1,000 square feet of living space and a double garage on a standard size lot near schools and shopping. By checking newspaper ads and talking with other rental owners, you find three generally comparable rentals.

> #1 has three bedrooms, one bath and 1100 square feet with a double garage and rents for $325 a month.
>
> #2 is two bedrooms, one bath with 800 square feet and a double garage that rents for $240 a month.
>
> #3 is a three bedroom home with 1,000 square feet in a poor neighborhood with no garage and it rents for $250 a month.

The best comparison is #1. Second best is #2 and by far the worst is #3. The only difference between your unit and #1 seems to be that it has 100 square feet—or about 10 percent—more space. The next one, #2, is 200 square feet smaller than yours (which would account for one less bedroom). #3 is not comparable—let's forget it.

Now for some math. Divide the rents by the square feet of #1 and #2 and you come up with a factor of 30¢ per square foot per month. If we multiply this factor by the 1,000 square feet in your unit, we arrive at a rent of $300 per unit per month by the Market Data Method.

The Cost Method

The third method of appraising rental price is by the COST METHOD. What would it cost the renter to buy this unit. For SFRs and smaller MFDs this figure should be about what your payments are to purchase it. If your unit is $40,000 and you put 10 percent down and signed a $36,000 mortgage at 9½ percent interest for 30 years, your payments would be $302.72 (principal and interest). Beyond this mortgage expense you have other expenses—but you also have the benefits of appreciation and tax savings to offset them. The Cost Method suggests a $300 a month rent. Of course, as the unit becomes older the mortgage payment stays the same. You must reevaluate rents by the Cost Method each year. Next year, what will this rental be worth and what would a renter's payments be to purchase it at the appreciated price?

You have set your rental for this unit at $300 a month based on information from the three methods of appraising rents: Income, Market Data and Cost. You have your rent set at a profitable and competitive rate to ensure you the best income and lowest vacancy rate available. Now let's learn about expenses.

How to Keep Expenses Down

The basic expenses—other than mortgage payment—you'll encounter with rentals are:

- Management
- Maintenance
- Vacancy loss

Keeping Management Costs Down

Management costs include the cost of collecting rents and keeping the units rented. Some rental owners hire property management firms to handle the day-to-day management of their units for a fee of from 5 to 10 percent of the gross rents. Other owners have a

HOW TO ACCELERATE EQUITIES

resident manager and still other owners of RI properties manage the units themselves. Until you are holding more than a half dozen rental units, doing it yourself is the best method. You'll learn how to cut costs better if you actually work with the tenants and units. It will also help you keep your management costs down. As your units become more numerous you can hire a resident manager or property management firm on a percentage basis.

Planning Ahead for Maintenance

Maintenance costs can be kept to a minimum by planning ahead. Schedule periodic maintenance and upkeep such as interior and exterior painting, plumbing inspection and roofing replacement on a rotating schedule so you can contract for them and get discount rates. Also, preventive maintenance ensures that maintenance is at a minimum. An overlooked leaking roof can cause expensive damage. Poor paint condition may cause a rise in vacancies.

Cutting Vacancy Losses to Zero

Finally, you can cut your vacancy rate to just about zero by doing these things:

- Require at least 20 days notice from tenants, or rents and deposits won't be refunded.
- Ask renters if you may show the unit to prospective renters while they are still living there. If so, offer them a concession on rents due or deposit returned.
- Place an ad in the paper as soon as you get or give notice to a tenant.
- Ask other renters if they know of someone looking for a place. If your tenants are leaving under amiable terms, ask them if they have any friends who have visited them and asked about renting it.
- Keep your rents at or below the rental market. It's much more profitable to take

ten dollars a month less than to have your unit vacant one or more months a year.

- Take care of your units. Have maintenance done when needed. Help your tenants keep them up. Keep them happy, stable and profitable.

How to Handle Problems

Handling renters doesn't have to be a problem. I've found that the longtime landlords have a rule about rental problems:

1. Answer problems quickly, and
2. Don't put up with *unprofitable* situations.

A client of mine, Hank L., owned a block of new homes that had poor insulation. Renters were complaining of high heating bills. As soon as Hank heard about it he checked with all of the renters to see if this were true. It was. All of the units were built by the same contractor, so that evening Hank called him to tell him that there was no insulation in the ceilings, which was required of all new construction. The contractor, interested in selling more units to Hank, was out the next afternoon to place insulation in all of the units.

When Hank contacted his renters he didn't promise to fix the problem—he only promised to check it out and get back to them as soon as he could. Now Hank's units are the best insulated ones in the neighborhood and his renters are satisfied—and making him money—because he dealt with the problem when it cropped up.

The second rule about rental problems is: don't put up with unprofitable situations. You purchased your RIs because you love *money*, not because you love *problems*. If you have a renter that has caused damage to a unit, evict him. If a renter is repeatedly late with the rent money, get rid of him and move a more responsible party in. If renters are disturbing other renters, ask them to move before you have a rash of vacant units. The dollars you lose because of nuisance or malicious renters are dollars out of your profit pocket.

How to Make Selective Improvements

One of the most profitable aspects of Accelerated Equities is increasing the value of your RI property with Selective Improvements. A Selective Improvement is an improvement made to a property that adds more value than its cost.

Profitable Selective Improvements include:

- Developing low maintenance landscaping
- Installing a low-cost privacy fence
- Painting the exterior of the unit
- Replacing damaged flooring or carpeting
- Painting interior walls
- Remodeling kitchen or bath
- Modernizing heating or lighting

To be profitable, Selective Improvements should cost no more than one-third of the increased value. As an example, if easy care landscaping will add $2,000 in value to your unit, plan to spend about $600 for the improvement. Never add an improvement that will only pay its way. Never add a fancy chain link fence costing $1500 to a home where the value would only increase $1500. That's not profitable Selective Improvements.

How to Selectively Improve the Yard

Whether you own SFRs or MFDs, the first thing your renters and visitors see is the public area of your yard. The public area is the portion visible from the street. This is the area that can make the best impression on renters and eventual purchasers. You can add many dollars of value to your unit by installing low-maintenance landscaping.

The first decision to make about landscaping is what type of ground cover you'll choose. The most popular, of course, is grass. Unfortunately, it is also the most difficult to maintain. Many RI unit owners are switching their landscaping to low maintenance ground covers such as rock, bark dust, gravel and easy-care plants like ivy and potentilla. The easier your yard is to maintain, the less trouble you'll have with renters keeping it up. And in the long run, low-maintenance landscaping is actually less expensive than other types of landscaping.

The next consideration is plants and bushes. Annuals require more care. Flowering perennials such as camelias, azaleas, rhododendrons and hydrangeas offer beauty, low cost and easy care. Shrubs are used to fence or break up portions of your yard. Ask your local nurseryman about the best plants and shrubs for your use.

Trees are the final consideration in choosing a low maintenance yard. Of course, if you already have large trees on the property, you may want to leave them where they are and design your low-maintenance yard around them. Otherwise your nurseryman will give you ideas on the best type of quick-growing, low-maintenance trees for your area and application.

The idea of low-maintenance Selective Improvements can be carried to the exterior of your Residential Income property. Decorative maintenance and repairs can add value to a unit as well as make it easier to rent. Smart investors consider quality paint an investment rather than an expense. A good paint job will add hundreds of dollars to the value of a run-down, below-market property. In fact, some RIs only need a fresh coat of paint to bring them to market value. Choose your color to complement neighboring structures, require low-maintenance and be a profitable improvement.

Trim can also add value. Inexpensive wooden shutters, accent painting or other trim offers a low-cost way to build the value of your unit.

Check the roofing on your RI unit. If it needs repairing, shop for a decorative style that will add value as well as practicality to your investment.

How to Selectively Improve the Interior of Your Residential Income Property

The idea of "cosmetic" Selective Improvements can be carried indoors profitably by painting walls, cabinets and ceilings as well as replacing flooring and modernizing fixtures.

HOW TO ACCELERATE EQUITIES

A few years ago Roger and Doris U., introduced to you earlier, purchased an older Cape Cod style home for just over $9,500. The renter they put in the unit helped them modernize the kitchen and bath, repaint the interior and exterior of the home and install new linoleum and carpet. They put a franklin fireplace in the corner of the living room and sold the unit for $24,900. Since they only spent $4,500 on materials, their profit—including labor—amounted to nearly $10,000. They made Selective Improvements to a home that was *under* market value because of deterioration and age—and made a healthy profit. You can do the same with any RI property—old or new, large or small—by making profitable Selective Improvements.

How to Profit from Other Accelerated Equity Techniques

There are many other ways you can add value to your Residential Income property through the use of Accelerated Equity techniques.

They include:

- Appreciation
- Depreciation
- Equity pay-off
- Packaging

Appreciation is the increase in value of a property because of inflation or demand. A good example of earning Accelerated Equity through appreciation is Donna S. in Chapter 4, who earned AE of $5,000 in her first year. Most of that increase in value came from appreciation. In recent years a 12 percent per year appreciation factor for RIs has been conservative. That's an increase of *one percent a month*—or about equal to the total monthly payment on the unit. Easy money.

Homes and RIs increase in value due to the law of supply and demand. In this world there is a limited supply of land. Especially land that is in locations where people want to live. Land in the frozen tundra of Canada and Alaska is inexpensive (without oil rights) because it is not near the conveniences of civilization and the comforts that most of us require. Land on Manhattan Island is very expensive because of supply and demand. There is a limited supply and a high demand by businesses and individuals.

Another reason for appreciation in value of real estate is inflation or the cost of replacement of structures. A building that cost $25,000 to build a few years ago may cost $45,000 to build today. The cost of building materials and labor has risen and has taken the cost of replacing a unit with it.

All of these factors work together *for the investor* as they increase the value of property faster than the general rate of inflation. Add to this the Power of Leverage and you can again see why RI properties make the best investment.

How to Depreciate Your Property for Extra Profits

Now I'm going to turn around and tell you that the value of real estate *goes down*. That's right. It's called *depreciation* and is the *theoretical* loss in value of a property because of deterioration and obsolescence. I said theoretical because—as you have seen—values actually go up. Actual depreciation is much slower than appreciation and is overcome by rising costs and values. Theoretical depreciation is what the government says you can take off your income tax as an *expense*. You don't have to pay taxes on it. This theoretical or book depreciation is why many people buy real estate. The "loss" on paper from this depreciation can be combined with their other income to show less income than they actually made. They "shelter" their other income—thus a property with a high amount of depreciation is called a "tax shelter."

There are a number of ways to depreciate your property. We'll discuss them here and in the next chapter as I tell you more about taxes. The three types of depreciation are:

- Straight Line Depreciation
- Accelerated Depreciation
- Component Depreciation

Straight Line Depreciation is where you have a building with an expected life of 20 years and you depreciate or deduct 1/20th of 100 percent or 5 percent of the cost per year as depreciation expense. With a $50,000 property this comes to $2,500 a year in nontaxable deduction. Land doesn't depreciate in value due to wear so it's not counted in figuring depreciation. And you can't depreciate your own home. It must be an investment property to qualify.

Accelerated Depreciation allows you to depreciate the property at a much faster rate than Straight Line. In the case of 200 percent Declining Balance Depreciation, the tax shelter is twice as much the first year as Straight Line Depreciation. And 150 percent Declining Balance is half again as much as Straight Line Depreciation. The disadvantage to these methods is that if you sell a property for more than the Accelerated Depreciation value, you may have to pay more taxes than if you claimed Straight Line Depreciation. I'll talk more about this in Chapter 6.

Component Depreciation may be the best way for the smart investor to take advantage of the tax shelter offered by allowable depreciation while not setting himself up for a tax penalty. The concept of Component Depreciation is simple: an RI may have a theoretical life of 40 years, but the carpets inside that home will theoretically only be good for seven years and the roof only ten years. The cost of each of these components—structure, carpets, appliances, roof, etc.—is estimated at the time of purchase, the depreciable life is set and each component is depreciated at a different rate. With Component Depreciation you actually have the advantages of both Straight Line Depreciation *and* Accelerated Depreciation without the risk of higher taxes for depreciating your property too quickly.

How to Accelerate Your Equity with Equity Payoff

One of the major advantages of holding RI property over other types of investments is the fact that while you are earning all of this money through Accelerated Equity techniques, someone else is paying your largest expense: your mortgage. If you are renting your unit for $275 a month and the mortgage payment, taxes and insurance total $270 you have a positive cash flow of just five dollars a month—but you're also earning the portion of your payment that goes toward the principal.

As an example, on a $40,000 mortgage at 9 percent interest for 30 years, the renters have earned you $280 in Equity Payoff the first year and $1,640 in the first five years. On a $40,000, 20 year mortgage at 9 percent they've earned you $360 the first year and $4,520 in the first five years. Rather than creating an expense, your renters are earning you *extra profits* through Equity Payoff. It's not the largest Accelerated Equity profit you'll make, but combined with other techniques Equity Payoff means extra cash in the pocket of the smart RI investor.

Making Higher Profits with Packaging

The final method of increasing the value of your RI property and thus accelerating your equity is with the technique called *Packaging*. Packaging is selling. It's merchandising.

The cost of manufacturing your favorite toothpaste is only a fraction of the price you pay for it. You are also paying for merchandising or Packaging. Through extensive radio, television and newspaper advertising, the toothpaste makers have shown us that we cannot survive socially without their toothpaste. The cost of this advertising campaign is added to the price of the toothpaste, and the benefits we feel we get from using it add value to the product in our eyes.

Even though this is an exaggerated example of how merchandising works, the same principle can be applied to renting real estate. By Packaging your RI property with "extras" you can not only pay for your campaign, but you can also increase the value of your property in the eyes of the potential renter. Here's an example of how one smart investor Packaged his RI for profit.

Manny V. Uses Productive Marketing Techniques

Manny V. owned a 12-plex near the college. It had been run down and over-priced when Manny took it over. He had an idea:

why not make his complex attractive to the college crowd? With a new paint job and some "cosmetics," Manny soon reopened his complex as the "Swinging Singles Apartments." Manny set up a recreation room with pool table and snack machines in one of the enclosed garages and was able to command greater rents.

Because of the demand for his units Manny was able to be more selective in choosing renters. He had fewer problems. At first he advertised units in the college paper, but he soon dropped it when the units filled up and vacancies were filled by word-of-mouth.

With the Accelerated Equity techniques of Packaging and Selective Improvements, Manny V. was able to turn a below-market RI into an above-market gold mine.

You'll learn more about Packaging a property for sale with Step 5 of my REAL ESTATE MILLIONAIRE PLAN coming up in the next chapter.

6

How to Add to Your Real Estate Profits with Productive Marketing

The Accelerated Equity techniques you've learned about thus far have given you "paper profits." In other words, the increased values you've earned through Selective Improvements, Equity Payoff and other AE techniques haven't been turned into cash yet. It's the difference between someone owing you $20 and having the $20 cash in your hand. Your net worth is still the same, but only the cash is spendable.

This chapter—the final step in the REAL ESTATE MILLIONAIRE PLAN—will show you exactly how to turn Accelerated Equity into spendable dollars with a minimum of effort, plus show you how to take advantage of tax laws to hold onto more of your dollars.

Charles and Barbara M. purchased their first Residential Income property three years ago. In that time they followed most of the Accelerated Equity techniques I've outlined for you. They found their Property with Potential through a FSBO, purchased it on a real estate contract using Creative Purchasing techniques and promptly increased its value with Selective Improvements, earning a rent increase of $25 per month per unit. Their $45,000 property increased in value to $67,500 in three years—but the $22,500 difference was just "paper profits" until they used Productive Marketing methods to turn their Accelerated Equity into cash.

They did so by selling the property on the open market. Using the PM techniques you'll soon learn about, Charles and Barbara sold their units within 30 days for a final price of $68,200. Their profit was the equity of $23,200 *plus* Equity Payoff of $2,200 *less* remodeling costs of $1,890, or $23,510—an increase of over 52 percent in three years (or over 17 percent a year).

That's excellent profits, but Charles and Barbara actually earned much more. Their down payment was 20 percent of the original price, or $9,000. For their investment of $9,000 they earned $23,510 in three years. That computes to a true return on their investment of 261 percent, or 87 percent per year—more than *10 times* what a bank would have paid them on their $9,000.

Fantastic, but true.

How to Cash in Your Chips

There are actually *two* methods of pulling your Accelerated Equity from a property:

- Sell the property
- Refinance the property

The first method, selling your RI, will bring you the highest and sometimes quickest return. You receive 100 percent of your equity less costs.

The second method, refinance, can sometimes be the most profitable overall because of Ramsey's Rule of Productive Marketing:

Never sell a winner!

In other words, if you have an RI property that is making you excellent income from rents and is easy to maintain, hang onto it. Take the property to a lending institution and borrow against your Accelerated Equity value, then pocket the cash for other investments while you let your RI continue to grow.

HOW TO ADD TO YOUR REAL ESTATE PROFITS

Productive Marketing is like owning a cow. If you have an unproductive cow you sell it—but if you have a productive one, you just sell the cream and keep the cow.

Deciding on Productive Marketing

Here are four questions you can ask yourself as you decide whether to keep the cow or the cream:

- What can I expect future income from this property to be?
- Will expenses of maintenance and operation remain the same, increase or decrease?
- How profitable will this RI property be in one year? Two years? Five?
- Do I need ready cash? How much? Should I sell the unit for the highest net figure or should I refinance for a lower net and a better overall return?

Indicators of when you should sell your RI include:

- A change in living trends in your area that may make your property less profitable.
- A need for the highest amount of cash to invest in other property.
- Too much Accelerated Equity in one property and not enough leverage.
- A strong "seller's market" for RI properties.

Okay. Let's first consider how to cash in on your Accelerated Equity by selling your property—then we'll look at the way you can refinance it profitably.

How to Sell Your RI Property Profitably

After you've built your Accelerated Equity to the point where you want to cash it in and take your profits, there are many things you can do to make your units more salable.

First, you can physically prepare your property for visitors. You can do "cosmetics" with touch-up painting, trimming lawns and shrubs, sweeping off roofs, setting out blooming flowers and hauling away any accumulated trash. Anything that will improve the potential buyer's first impressions of your property will also improve your chances of a quick, easy and profitable sale.

Another part of Productive Marketing is getting your rental records in order. As a fellow investor, your potential buyer is interested in the same things you were when you bought your RI property:

- How much are the rents?
- Have they been increased lately?
- Are they above or below average market?
- What is your vacancy factor?
- What are your management costs?
- Is there a positive cash flow at your suggested sales price?
- How much?

Income Opportunity Fact Sheet

Many successful RI property sellers make up what I call an "Income Opportunity Fact Sheet" for the property they plan to sell. They give copies to interested buyers. It includes basic information on the property, units, taxes, rent rolls, vacancy, expenses, price terms available and suggested methods of purchasing.

Remember to talk with your tenants about showing your property. On an SFR you should ask their permission to show the interior of the home. On MFDs you can show the manager's apartment or get permission from one of the tenants to make his the model unit. If necessary, a buyer can make an offer "subject to satisfactory inspection" of the rental units.

Once you've made your RI property ready to sell—and you've set your price using the methods outlined in previous REMAP steps—there are four ways of promoting your opportunity:

Talk with other investors. As you've bought and studied local property you've probably met other investors who are interested in buying additional RI property. Keep their names and phone numbers as potential clients for your units.

Advertise locally. Place an ad in the closest daily newspaper under "Income Property For Sale." Rather than lead with the price, start your ad with statements like "Six units on low-down contract" or "Rental house with excellent net returns."

Advertise regionally and nationally. Depending on the size of your RI property, you can sometimes bring in buyers from other areas with an ad in a metropolitan newspaper such as *The Los Angeles Times, The Denver Post, The Chicago Tribune, The New York Times* or *The Seattle Times.*

Contact a Realtor. Many investors work exclusively through their own Realtor. In fact, you should consider giving a Realtor an "open" or "exclusive" listing on your property. He is a good source of qualified buyers.

How to Sell on the Best Terms

There are three ways you can sell your RI property—and the best one depends on your own needs and reasons for selling. The three methods are:

- Cash
- Wrap-Around
- Soft-Money Mortgage

Let's consider them individually.

The "Cash" Method

"Cash" means that you receive a lump sum of cash for your equity in the property. This can be done by a purchaser who offers you all cash or by a purchaser who offers you a cash down payment plus cash from the proceeds of a loan he will get on the property. It's all cash to you.

Clinton J. and Tom H. sold their RI property to Stan M. for

$135,000. Stan put $27,000 of his own money down and borrowed the balance of $108,000 from a mortgage company. Stan pays $1,007.64 a month to the mortgage company for the next 20 years. Clinton and Tom receive the entire purchase price in cash at the time of closing—20 percent from Stan and 80 percent from the mortgage company.

Of course, this offer was written "subject to the purchaser obtaining 80 percent financing" on the property. That means that if Stan didn't get the loan he wouldn't be obligated to buy the property and would be refunded his earnest money. Selling property subject to financing takes more time than having a purchaser walk up and plop down the entire purchase price in cash, but Clinton and Tom realize that an "all cash" buyer is very rare—especially in RI property where buyers are using the Power of Leverage.

The Wrap-Around Method

A Wrap-Around Mortgage is a second mortgage which is "wrapped around" the first mortgage. In other words, the seller takes a second mortgage on the property and is responsible for payments on the first mortgage. He collects the entire payment from the buyer.

Here's an example: A 12-unit complex that sold for $180,000 a few years ago has been increased in value through Accelerated Equity techniques to a value of $300,000. The current mortgage balance is $140,000 at 8 percent interest. The payments are $1,255.50 a month. The seller offers his property on a Wrap-Around Mortgage under these terms:

- $300,000 purchase price with
- $60,000 down and
- $2,318.40 a month for 20 years at 10 percent interest

How much is the seller making?

- $120,000 in Accelerated Equity ($300,000 less $180,000)
- $60,000 of it in cash at closing

HOW TO ADD TO YOUR REAL ESTATE PROFITS

- $60,000 of it collected from the second mortgage at 10 percent interest for 20 years
- Plus 2 percent interest on $180,000 for about 20 years (difference between 8 percent paid on current mortgage and 10 percent earned on Wrap-Around by seller)

So the purchaser gives the seller $60,000 in cash at closing and pays him $2,318.40 a month. Out of this the seller pays the first mortgage holder $1,255.50 a month. The seller's net each month is the difference of $1,062.90 for 20 years. Not bad.

The Soft Money Mortgage

The third method of cashing in on Accelerated Equity in your Residential Income property is by selling it with a "Soft Money Mortgage." A "Hard Money Mortgage" is one where money actually transfers from the buyer to the seller at closing. In a "Soft Money Mortgage," the seller offers his equity—or part of it—in exchange for monthly payments.

There are two types of Soft Money Mortgages: Real Estate Contracts and Purchase Money Mortgages. In a Real Estate Contract the seller retains title to the property until the property is paid off. A Purchase Money Mortgage gives the buyer title to the property and puts a mortgage or lien on the property in favor of the seller.

Johnny D. has sold many of his rental properties to other investors on Real Estate Contracts. One was sold to Henry and Florence T. who wanted it for their first RI property. It was a remodeled older home with a purchase price of $42,000. Johnny owned it free and clear. He took 10 percent down ($4,200) and had the purchasers sign a Real Estate Contract for the balance of $37,800. The down payment was the only cash that changed hands at closing, and Henry and Florence made their monthly payments directly to Johnny who continued to hold legal title. If the buyers defaulted on their contract, Johnny got the property back quickly.

If they had signed a Purchase Money Mortgage, the title would be in the name of Henry and Florence T. and Johnny would hold the mortgage as security. In case of default, Johnny would have to start court action to get the title back.

As you can see, the Purchase Money Mortgage is made more in favor of the purchaser than the Real Estate Contract. Otherwise, there is little difference.

How to Refinance Your Property Profitably

What if you don't want to sell your property. What if you've accepted Ramsey's Rule of Productive Marketing:

Never sell a winner!

and want to keep your RI property—but still want to pull your Accelerated Equity out of it and use it for other investments. Then it's time to consider *refinancing*.

One of the major advantages of refinancing a winning RI is that the money you receive from the equity is virtually *tax free*—until you sell the property. If you were to sell it under the methods just outlined, you might have to pay taxes on your profit. But you can use the proceeds from your refinance without paying taxes on it for a while.

Another reason for refinancing is to prepare for a sale of your property. One example of this I was involved in concerned a limited partnership called Semlo Investments, which used Accelerated Equity techniques to increase a property's value from $110,000 to $200,000 in just one year. Their mortgage on the property was $75,000. They refinanced the property for 80 percent of its new value—or $160,000—then sold it to another investment group for $200,000 with $40,000 down, and assumed the new mortgage. By doing this, Semlo Investments not only got quick cash for their equity, but they also made it easier for the purchaser to buy their property.

How to Set-Up Conventional Refinancing

A conventional refinance means that the property is refinanced through conventional methods (see REMAP STEP 2—Chapter 3). Depending on the lending institution, the current money market

HOW TO ADD TO YOUR REAL ESTATE PROFITS

and other factors, many conventional lenders will refinance for 80 percent of the property's appraised value. By using conventional refinancing methods, you won't be able to draw out all of your Accelerated Equity, but you will be able to use it as a source of additional Breeding Funds.

You can also refinance your RI property by securing a second mortgage against the property. By doing this, you leave the original or first mortgage intact. The disadvantage is that second mortgage interest rates are usually higher than first mortgage interest rates—seconds are considered riskier by lending institutions.

Loretta P. bought her first investment property for $28,000 with just $2,800 down and a $25,200 first mortgage. After using Accelerated Equity techniques she increased its value to $40,000. The equity she had in the property then totaled about $14,800 and she was easily able to secure a second mortgage for 80 percent of that equity—or $11,840. Loretta used the proceeds of her second mortgage to pay back her original investment of $2,800, and she had about $9,000 left to use for her next RI opportunity.

The best part was that Loretta still had her first investment property. She kept the cow and sold the cream.

How to Profit from Tax Planning

The average taxpayer only thinks about the taxes he must pay on April 15th.

The smart real estate investor starts tax planning 15½ months earlier—on January 1 of the tax year. Why? Because he knows that smart tax planning can save him hundreds and even thousands of spendable dollars.

Taxes are money demanded by the government for its support or for a specific service. Taxes are levied on things of value such as incomes, sales and real property. In this book we're most interested in taxes on the income from real property and how you can legally pay the least amount possible. Your accountant is the best source of information on specific tax questions, but in the next few pages I'll try to outline some of the things you should know about as you increase your taxable income on your way to becoming a real estate millionaire.

Basically, there are two kinds of income recognized by the Internal Revenue Service:

- Ordinary Income
- Capital Gains

Ordinary Income includes income from your job, a gift or lottery winning and other ordinary sources. Capital Gains is the gain or profit made from the sale of a capital or long-term asset held for more than twelve months. Only one-half of the net long-term Capital Gain is taxable.

As an example, if you were to earn $20,000 from your regular job and another $20,000 from the sale of one of your income-producing properties, the tax you must pay would be only half as much on the Capital Gain as on the Ordinary Income. This is just one more reason why real estate is the best investment you can make.

Taking Title

There are three phases to RI property ownership and each has special tax considerations. The phases are:

- Origination
- Operation
- Termination

The first factor to consider in Origination, or buying a property, is the method of ownership. There are many ways you can take title to your property and each has a different effect on your tax status. Before you take title, you should consult your attorney and accountant, but generally these are the types and characteristics of ownership:

- *Individual*—as an individual (a single man, a single woman, a widow, a widower, a married man as his separate estate, etc.) you must usually report profits or losses from property as part of your income. Your liability for debts contracted because of your income property (bills, mortgage, suits) is not limited to that property, but can be attached to other property you own.

- *Tenancy in Common* or *Community Property*—as a married couple your taxation and liability are the same as an individual.

- *Limited Partnership*—is a partnership of "general" and "limited" partners where the general partners have both a voice in management and a liability for debts while limited partners are money sources and have no voice in management and no debt liability beyond their investment in the properties. Income is taxed on the individual partners.

- *Corporations*—taxation is double: the IRS taxes the profits of the corporation and taxes the owners when the profits are disbursed. The advantage of a corporation is that losses and indebtedness cannot be passed on to the corporate owners. They have limited liability.

- *Other*—there are other methods of taking title to property such as general partnerships, real estate investment trusts and cooperatives, but these are of little interest to the new RI investor.

Smaller income properties are normally purchased by individuals or tenants in common. Medium sized investments are often made by limited partnerships or small corporations. Most large income properties are purchased by corporations for liability reasons.

Another factor that is important to taxation is acquisition costs. How much does it cost you to buy your RI property? These acquisition costs—attorney fees, brokerage fees, closing costs and repairs—are tax-deductible expenses. Keep track of them because they will not only be deductible expenses, but they will also be charged against your costs of origination or buying the property and can be deducted from Capital Gains.

A third factor to remember as you buy your RI properties is that interest is a tax-deductible expense. In fact, it will probably be your largest on-going expense. Keep a close record of interest and points paid. As an example, payments on a $100,000 mortgage for ten years at 10 percent interest are $1,321.57 a month. During the first month $833.34—or 63 percent of the payment—goes toward interest and is a tax-deductible expense.

Tax Considerations on Operation

As you operate your RI property for profit, there will be ways to legally minimize your taxes. The most important is one that has already been discussed: depreciation. Let's take another look at it from the tax standpoint.

Depreciation, as you remember, is setting aside money to replace a property because of wear and tear, decay or loss of value from time that make it less valuable. Normally, property owners don't actually set money aside—because property doesn't actually go down in value—but they can still use depreciation as an expense. Here are the different methods of depreciating RI property:

- *Straight Line Method*—Annual depreciation is calculated by dividing the depreciable basis by the years of useful life.
- *Declining Balance Method*—The amount of depreciation is subtracted from the remaining balance before computing the next year's depreciation. This is also known as accelerated depreciation. Declining Balance Methods use 125, 150 or 200 percent of the Straight Line Method each year. Another type of Declining Balance, Sum-of-the-years-digits, is rarely used.

The Internal Revenue Service currently recognizes these methods and applications for depreciating RI properties:

New Residential Buildings   Straight Line
                                            Declining Balance:
                                              125%, 150%, 200%
                                              Sum-of-the-years-digits

HOW TO ADD TO YOUR REAL ESTATE PROFITS

Used Residential Buildings Straight Line
(with more than 20 years Declining Balance:
of remaining life) 125%

With Component Depreciation—discussed in Chapter 5—normal depreciation on components is:

Roof	10 years
Air conditioning	10 years
Carpets	7 years
Appliances	7 years
Doors and windows	15 years

Tax Considerations on Termination

Tax-wise, the sale of your RI property is probably the most important part of ownership. Here are the things you should consider as you sell your AE property:

Are you a *dealer* or an *investor*? A dealer is someone who purchases property primarily for resale. Income earned by a dealer is taxable as Ordinary Income. An investor is one who purchases property to hold as an income-producing investment. Income from the sale of an investor's property is taxed as Capital Gains—half the tax rate the dealer has to pay. Talk with your accountant, but do everything you can to remain an investor rather than a dealer. A dealer is a speculator. An investor is a builder.

Recapture is a bad word to the smart investor. Recapture is when the IRS comes back and charges tax on property you've sold at the Ordinary Income rate rather than at the Capital Gain rate. Why should they do this? Because you depreciated your property too fast. The recapture provision says that the gain made in a sale that's the excess between accelerated and normal depreciation can be taxed at the higher Ordinary Income rate. This can be costly.

Most investors avoid the problem of recapture by using Straight Line or Component Depreciation rather than Accelerated Depreciation on their RIs. This allows you to normally call any cash made a Capital Gain and have it taxed at half the rate of Ordinary Income.

Adjusted Basis is another consideration when you sell your income property. Adjusted Basis is the amount of taxable gain figured by subtracting the basis—or cost of a property—from the net proceeds of the sale.

If you purchased a property for $40,000 and the cost of buying it was $2,000, your Adjusted Basis is $42,000. Then if you sell the property for $60,000, your Adjusted Tax Basis is $18,000. You'll pay Capital Gains tax on $18,000 rather than $20,000.

Delaying Your Tax Obligation

Smart investors who have minimized the taxes they must pay will also use other profitable techniques of the REAL ESTATE MILLIONAIRE PLAN to legally put off paying some of that tax for awhile. There are three ways you can legally put off taxes—two of them are very important to the RI owner. I'll give you examples of each as you progress through your Wealth Years in the coming chapters. Here are the methods:

- *Installment Sale*—Tax laws state that if no more than 30 percent of the selling price is received by the seller during the year of the sale, the seller may qualify for installment sale accounting. In other words, if the seller takes a Real Estate Contract and accepts 29 percent down (to be safe) and is paid the balance in installments, the Capital Gain is taxed during the year it is received rather than at the time of the sale. Result: lower taxes.

- *Exchange*—In a tax-deferred exchange, property owners can exchange their equity in one property for equity in a similar property without paying taxes on the exchange until the property is finally sold. Taxes are still due, but the payment is deferred until later.

- *Sale of Principal Residence*—Capital Gain on the sale of your own home can be deferred if you buy another home of equal or higher cost within a

HOW TO ADD TO YOUR REAL ESTATE PROFITS

specified time after the sale. This tax-deferment is primarily for the homebuyer and of little interest to the investor.

As you can see, the smart RI investor doesn't wait until taxes are due to think about them. He begins looking at his tax obligation *before* it is an obligation so he can take advantage of the legally acceptable methods of paying the least taxes—or deferring payment until later and using the cash for more investments.

The Real Estate Millionaire Plan Will Take You to Your Goal

That's it. That's how the Five Steps of the REAL ESTATE MILLIONAIRE PLAN can bring you wealth and success. REMAP is an easy-to-follow system of building your wealth with a simple investment formula:

$$PWP \times IF + CP \times AE + PM = SP$$

Or, PROPERTY WITH POTENTIAL MULTIPLIED BY IMAGINATIVE FINANCING PLUS CREATIVE PURCHASING MULTIPLIED BY ACCELERATED EQUITY PLUS PRODUCTIVE MARKETING EQUALS SUBSTANTIAL PROFITS.

The REAL ESTATE MILLIONAIRE PLAN is based on actual case histories and practical methods used by real estate millionaires throughout the country. In the coming chapters you will see how many people like yourself have used the REAL ESTATE MILLIONAIRE PLAN to build their fortunes in profitable WEALTH STAGES.

Let's get started.

7

Using Leverage in SFRs as Real Estate Profit Starting Blocks

Welcome to the most profitable years of your life.

You've set a financial goal of building your personal wealth to a specific number of dollars within the next few years—and you've decided to do it with the world's best investment: Residential Income real estate.

Your method of building your fortune is one that has been used by hundreds of millionaires and multimillionaires: the REAL ESTATE MILLIONAIRE PLAN. REMAP shows you how you can reach your financial goal simply and easily. With it you can make $100,000 in one year, $1,000,000 in four years, $3,000,000 in ten years, $500,000 in six years or any other realistic goal you set.

This book will show you exactly how to reach the specific goal of making your *first quarter million in five years*. Many of the examples you'll read are built around this realistic goal—but every technique and every principle will work just as well with any other goal you set. The REAL ESTATE MILLIONAIRE PLAN is a *flexible system* designed to be adapted to the personal needs of each user.

Along the way you'll meet many people much like yourself who have decided to reach out for a higher level of living by applying the successful techniques of real estate millionaires. One such couple will show you step-by-step how they built their fortune with my REAL ESTATE MILLIONAIRE PLAN. Others will illustrate special techniques you'll be able to quickly apply to your own situation and turn your dreams into realities.

Building Your Real Estate Fortune in Wealth Stages

Whatever your final financial goal, you can reach it quickly and easily by setting up your own WEALTH STAGES—stepping stones that will bridge the gap between where you are today and the goal you want to reach. In each WEALTH STAGE you'll set a higher goal. In each WEALTH STAGE you'll use more refined and more sophisticated techniques to make your goal a spendable reality. In each WEALTH STAGE you'll learn more about the opportunities and profits available in buying, holding and selling Residential Income real estate in your own city or town.

How One Young Couple Developed Their Real Estate Millionaire Plan into Wealth Stages

To illustrate the WEALTH STAGES and to show you how a typical investor can earn his first quarter million dollars in real estate in five years or less, I'll introduce you to Kevin and Dianne Simpson.

Kevin is 32 years old, married with two young girls. He works in the pot room of an aluminum plant and makes a good wage. But Kevin and his wife, Dianne, decided that they wanted more from life than a 40-hour-a-week job and a regular check. They wanted the spare time and money to travel—to take their children to Hawaii and the South Seas on an extended vacation. They wanted a piece of the Good Life.

I introduced the REAL ESTATE MILLIONAIRE PLAN to Kevin and Dianne just as I'm doing to you. Their goal was the same

USING LEVERAGE IN SFRS   127

one suggested by this book—to make more than $250,000 in equity within five years by buying, operating and selling Residential Income real estate. Their successes and mistakes—along with those of dozens of other very average people—will illustrate how you can build your own fortune in WEALTH STAGES.

The Simpsons decided to reach their $250,000-five-year goal by starting with a Breeding Fund of $8,000 and *doubling* it every year for five years or five WEALTH STAGES. You'll see others start with *no capital* and still reach the same realistic goal.

Getting Your Fortune Started Today

Here's how the Simpsons came up with their Breeding Fund of $8,000 that would soon become more than $250,000:

KEVIN AND DIANNE'S BREEDING FUND

Savings ($4,000 balance—put half in Fund)	$2,000
Signature Loan (based on income from job)	$3,000
Sold second car (not being used)	$2,000
Promissory Note (to themselves: $100 mo. for 10 mo.)	$1,000
TOTAL BREEDING FUND AVAILABLE FOR INVESTING	$8,000

Kevin and Dianne had $8,000—$7,000 in cash and a $1,000 promissory note at $100 a month for 10 months. They decided to use only half of their savings for the Breeding Fund in case of other emergencies. That's smart thinking. Their signature loan cost them more than their savings account interest paid, but the loan helped them build their credit rating.

Another smart REMAP investor, Steve L., started his real estate fortune with *zero dollars* in his Breeding Fund. He used a technique I showed you back in Chapter 3—100 percent Financing—to get things rolling. He made out a financial statement and took it around to the banks and mortgage companies in his area, telling the loan officers that he would quickly assume any repossessed properties. He knew that most banks aren't set up to hold repossessed homes very long and would much rather have someone assume a delinquent mortgage than go through the time and trouble of putting it back on the marketplace and losing many months of payments.

Within three weeks, Steve had calls from two different banks for repossessions. He checked both of them out, approved them and signed the paperwork. The same week he had renters in each that were paying more than the mortgage payments in rent. Using Accelerated Equity techniques he built equity by $10,000 each in the first year. Starting with *no capital*, Steve made a profit—after expenses—of over $18,000 in one short year.

The point is, whether your Breeding Fund is $8,000, $3,000 or zero dollars, start moving with your REAL ESTATE MILLIONAIRE PLAN *right now*.

Wealth Stage 1

It's here. This is the first of your five WEALTH STAGES and it's ready to make you money. Your goal for WEALTH STAGE 1 is not a *quarter million dollars*. It's a much easier goal and one that you'll quickly reach. Your goal in this first WEALTH STAGE is to turn your Breeding Fund into $16,000. That's it. Time after time in the first six chapters of this book you've seen average people make 100 percent, 200 percent and more on their RI investment in one year or less. You can do even better because you know how to apply the REAL ESTATE MILLIONAIRE PLAN.

And you're going to start building your fortune with the type of Residential Income property you are most familiar with—SFRs or Single Family Residences.

Why are SFRs your best first investment?

- Because SFRs offer you safety and liquidity. Single Family Residences are easy to buy, easy to maintain and easy to sell. They offer low risk and high profits.

- Because SFRs offer Accelerated Equity. Single Family Residences not only bring in income each month, but also increase in value due to demand, inflation and rising building costs. SFR RIs also offer savings on income taxes due to tax-deductible expenses and depreciation.

USING LEVERAGE IN SFRS

- Because SFRs offer you leverage. You can purchase your first Single Family Residence RI property for a lower down payment than is needed on other types of RIs.

- Because SFRs offer you better renters. The people who rent SFRs are usually families with their own furniture and some appliances. They are more established and usually offer the new RI owner less headaches than the MFD or apartment dweller.

Investing in SFRs offers you the best parts of RI property investment: lower risk, higher growth factor, lower down payment and fewer headaches. Most real estate millionaires started with Single Family Residences.

How to Choose Your First SFR

What kind of SFR should you buy first? And how? Well, your first RI property should be a "trainer"—one that will help you reach your first WEALTH STAGE goal of building your investment to $16,000 *plus* one that will help you learn how to profit with the REAL ESTATE MILLIONAIRE PLAN.

Your first SFR should require only moderate Selective Improvements. You should be able to increase its value with paint and landscaping, but unless you have experience in construction, it's best not to get into SFRs that need a lot of fixing up your first time out.

You'll also be looking for a first SFR where the seller is highly motivated to sell so you can use the Power of Leverage to your best advantage.

How the Simpsons Find Their First Profitable Property with Potential

Kevin and Dianne Simpson used techniques offered in Chapter 2 to find their first Property with Potential. They used the five steps to finding a profitable real estate investment:

- LEARN exactly how real estate profits are made;
- SEARCH for properties that fit these requirements and help you complete your financial goals;
- CHECK each potential purchase to authenticate facts and figures;
- ANALYZE each real estate opportunity; and
- DECIDE on the best action to take.

The Simpsons spent many weeks combing the newspaper classified ads to get an idea of how much SFRs were selling for and how much they were bringing in the rental marketplace.

Another smart investor, Paul T., kept up with the rental market in his town by placing a map of the area on one wall and marking rentals advertised in the paper. He used flags to show the number of bedrooms, rent asked and whether it was a house or apartment. Paul soon learned that most of the SFR rentals were concentrated into a six square block area in his town. The area was near schools and shopping.

A check at the courthouse showed that the units were owned by half a dozen investors and most had been held for about five years. Paul knew that these investors must have a large equity in these RIs by now, so he called each one of them and offered to buy any of the units on low-down-payment contracts so the sellers wouldn't have to pay such high taxes on their capital gain.

Within three weeks Paul had purchased four of these units—one with no down payment—and was on his way to his personal goal of $100,000 in two years with the REAL ESTATE MILLIONAIRE PLAN.

Checking Out Property with Potential to Ensure the Best Investment

Kevin and Dianne searched for their PWPs in the daily newspapers. One weekend they found three SFR opportunities they wanted to inspect. To show you how it's done, let's see how they checked these units out for potential.

The first unit the Simpsons inspected—which we'll call *Oppor-*

USING LEVERAGE IN SFRS 131

tunity A—was a preowned home offered by a couple getting a divorce. It was a three bedroom home in a fair rental area about four miles from major shopping. It was in good condition and offered them the potential of a few profitable Selective Improvements.

At my suggestion Kevin completed a PROPERTY PRICING SHEET, as you saw in Chapter 2, and came up with a fair market value of $39,000. The sellers said they must have $41,000 in order to complete the financial end of their divorce. They were obviously motivated sellers.

Opportunity B looked better from the start. It was also a three bedroom SFR that had been previously used as a rental property and was located in the center of a high-demand rental area. It was a newer home. The price was $40,000 with an assumable $32,000 mortgage. It needed only a few Selective Improvements, but Kevin and Dianne felt that they could be done profitably and raise the value of the RI quickly and easily.

Opportunity C seemed even better. It was an older home in an established neighborhood where most of the units were rentals. There were many Selective Improvement opportunities. The unit was offered on a real estate contract at the prevailing interest rate with just $5,000 down on a $40,000 purchase price—which their PROPERTY PRICING SHEET said was right at market value.

How could the Simpsons make an accurate comparison of the relative value of these opportunities and choose the best one?

Using An SFR Investment Rating Guide to Find the Best Property with Potential

Let me introduce you to one of the handiest methods of finding the right SFR for you. I call it my SFR INVESTMENT RATING GUIDE and it offers a simple method of comparing separate Properties with Potential to help you decide on the *best opportunity* based on the four most important factors to the smart investor:

- Location
- Condition
- Price and Terms
- Profitability

It can work for you.

SRF INVESTMENT RATING GUIDE

LOCATION	Excellent rental area	5
	Very good rental area	4
	Good rental area	3
	Fair rental area	2
	Poor rental area	1
CONDITION	High number of profitable SIs	5
	Good number of profitable SIs	4
	Fair number of profitable SIs	3
	Very few profitable SIs	2
	No profitable SIs available	1
PRICE/TERMS	Priced below market/excellent terms	5
	Priced below market/fair terms	4
	Priced at market/excellent terms	3
	Priced at market/fair terms	2
	Priced above market/average terms	1
PROFITABILITY	Excellent AE and leverage	5
	Very good AE and leverage	4
	Good AE and leverage	3
	Fair AE and leverage	2
	Poor AE and leverage	1

TOTAL SFR INVESTMENT RATING POINTS (possible 20) _____

Of course, your rating of RI opportunities is a relative thing and each investor will rate each opportunity differently, but what you're most interested in is a method of comparing separate opportunities. This RATING GUIDE can be modified to fit special requirements. Most important, it offers a system for helping you decide on the best Property with Potential.

How One Investor Used the SFR Investment Rating Guide

The Simpsons used this RATING GUIDE to decide on the best opportunity for them. With it they came up with these scores:

USING LEVERAGE IN SFRS

Opportunity A   9 points
Opportunity B   14 points
Opportunity C   15 points

The RATING GUIDE showed them that Opportunities B and C were both very profitable and that Opportunity A was weak in comparison. Even so, the Simpsons didn't want to rule any of them out until they considered each of them thoroughly.

Imaginative Financing and the Power of Leverage

As you've seen, the Power of Leverage is one of the greatest powers in the REAL ESTATE MILLIONAIRE PLAN. It gives the smart investor the opportunity to take a return of 10, 15 or 25 percent and multiply it into a return on his initial investment of 100 percent, 200 percent and more in a short time.

The Power of Leverage is developed by making profit not only on your own money, but also on *Rented Money*. It's borrowing money at 9, 10 and even 12 percent interest and making *double* or even *triple* that return on it by investing it safely in RI property.

Making Big Money with Leverage Ratios

A *Leverage Ratio* is the relationship between your investment and the amount of Rented Money it can draw. Here's an example:

Foster M. found an excellent SFR in a good rental area and he was ready to buy it. The price was $36,000. He estimated a down payment of $3,600 and closing costs of about $400 for a total investment of $4,000 of his own money. With this $4,000 he hoped to attract enough Rented Money to purchase the income-producing home: $32,400. If he could, Foster would have a Leverage Ratio of 8.1 to 1. In other words, every one of his dollars would be able to attract $8.10 in Rented Money. The higher the Leverage Ratio, the larger his profit.

Foster got the loan, purchased the SFR and sold it two years later for $45,000. A profit of 25 percent in two years? Much better than that. Foster earned a $9,000 equity increase in two years with an investment of just $4,000—that's a *112½ percent increase* on his original investment *every year.*

You can do as well or better if you use Leverage Ratios in deciding on the best SFR investment.

How the Simpsons Used Leverage Ratios to Find the Most Profitable Opportunity

As you remember, the Simpson's Opportunity A was a preowned home with a market value estimated at $39,000 where the sellers said they must have $41,000. Let's see how Kevin and Dianne could use Leverage Ratios and the Power of Leverage to purchase this SFR at $40,000.

First, they would have to give the sellers cash for their home, which means the Simpsons would have to get a conventional mortgage on it. Most banks require at least 20 percent down on a nonowner occupied house mortgage, and the sellers indicated they weren't interested in taking a second mortgage back. They wanted all cash. That means that Kevin and Dianne would have to come up with $8,000 in cash plus closing costs of about $1,400—a total of $9,400—to get a $32,000 mortgage. That's a Leverage Ratio of 3.4 to 1. That is, for every $1.00 they invested they would be able to rent $3.40. Not very good.

Opportunity B was a rental priced at $40,000 with an assumable $32,000 mortgage that scored high on their SFR INVESTMENT RATING GUIDE. If Kevin and Dianne were able to assume the mortgage, there would only be about $300 in closing costs and they would need $8,300 in cash to earn $32,000 in Rented Money. That's a Leverage Ratio of 3.85 to 1. It's better than Opportunity A, but still not high enough to be called a Golden Opportunity.

The Simpsons thought about it a little more. What if they could talk the sellers of Opportunity B into taking a second mortgage for $4,300. Then they would only have to come up with $4,000 to rent $36,300—a Leverage Ratio of about 9 to 1. Very good.

Opportunity C was a preowned home with many Selective Improvement opportunities. It was listed at $40,000 on a real estate contract with $5,000 down. Closing costs, they estimated, would be about $300 and their total out-of-pocket costs would be $5,300 to rent $35,000 in equity. That's a Leverage Ratio of 6.6 to 1. Not as good, but still impressive.

Based on the findings of their SFR INVESTMENT RATING GUIDE, their Leverage Ratios and their own personal investment goals, Kevin and Dianne Simpson made Opportunity B their first choice and Opportunity C their second choice as their initial Property with Potential.

Using Creative Purchasing Techniques to Ensure a Profit on Your First SFR

Buying right is often more important than selling right. A small investor knows that if he buys right, he is assured of a profit when he sells whether the market is up or down.

You can make sure you buy your Residential Income properties right by following the REAL ESTATE MILLIONAIRE PLAN and using the techniques you've learned. You can guarantee yourself a healthy profit on every transaction by doing these things:

- *Keep the pressure off yourself.* Don't be forced into buying *any* property. Know what profit you can make on the transaction, but never feel that this is the only opportunity you'll have. It isn't. The REAL ESTATE MILLIONAIRE PLAN will give you many more. Never let the seller—or anyone else—high pressure you.

- *Put the pressure on the seller.* Know why the seller is selling and remind him of the opportunity you are offering him. Show him how your offer will be to his best benefit. Sell yourself and your offer to him.

- *Know the value of what you're buying.* Never buy a "pig in a poke." Take time to analyze the property and its profitability before you make an offer. Ensure a profit for yourself before you ever buy.

- *Write your own terms.* Based on your funds, desired leverage and available financing, make an offer with the best terms for yourself. Sellers are more interested in price; buyers in terms.

- *Use Creative Purchasing techniques to negotiate the best deal.* As you present your offer, get approval from the seller on minor points, find similarities in yours and the seller's needs, minimize the things that separate you from agreement and use the See-Saw technique of trading concessions in negotiating.

If you'll follow these five rules of Creative Purchasing, you'll *guarantee* yourself a profit on every RI property you buy.

How a Country Boy Made Big Money in the City

Hiram V. was a slow-talking country boy from Arkansas. He left school early and very few people who met him ever realized that he was worth over *$1.2 million.* How did he amass this fortune? By buying, holding and selling Residential Income real estate.

Hiram was at his best when he was negotiating. He put pressure on a seller as few men could. When Hiram was ready to make an offer on a property, he would approach the seller and start questioning him about the property, then change the subject as soon as he could. He would let the seller know that he was interested, but he wanted the seller to make the first move.

Sometimes this "cat and mouse" game went on for hours before the seller would ask if he wanted to make an offer. Hiram would always answer, "Well, that depends. What's the least you'll take for it?" This question usually gave Hiram a lower starting point than the asking price. Then, to not offend the seller he would say something like, "If you say that's a fair price, I guess it is—but it just isn't worth that much to me."

Almost invariably, the seller would then ask, "What did you have in mind" and Hiram would pull out a pencil and start figuring. He usually deducted about 20 percent from the seller's low starting point, but it somehow took him as much as ten minutes to double-check his figures and announce them to the seller. Meanwhile, the seller waited.

Once the two settled on the price Hiram would continue, "Of course, that's if I can pay you on terms. For $2,000 less I'll give it to you in cash," and Hiram would pull out a roll of bills. Most of the sellers wanted cash and he often got the price reduction. If they agreed he would give them a few thousand dollars in cash and tell them he wanted to close the transaction within 30 days and that he would have the balance at closing.

Then Hiram would go to his bank and borrow the balance of what he needed and secure it with a mortgage on the property. He used the Power of Leverage.

Most important, he used Creative Purchasing to keep the pressure off himself and on the seller. He also wrote his own terms. Hiram guaranteed himself a profit by buying under market value and on the best terms possible.

Hiram was no dummy.

How Kevin and Dianne Used Creative Purchasing to Make an Offer on Their PWP

The Simpsons decided to make an offer on Opportunity B first, hoping that the sellers would give them a second mortgage for $4,300 so they could assume the existing loan with only $4,000 in cash.

First, the couple made out an INCOME ANALYSIS SHEET on the opportunity to check the profitability of the purchase. Then they developed a PRO-CON SHEET to make certain they were aware of all of the advantages and disadvantages of the transaction. They wanted to make sure they were in love with the mathematics of the opportunity and not just the property itself.

Finally, Kevin and Dianne sat down to consider the seller's motivation. They put themselves in the seller's shoes. They knew that the seller, a doctor, had taken a position in a hospital in another part of the state and that he wanted to sell the property before moving in two months. They also understood that, if he didn't sell the unit by then, he might put it in the hands of a property management firm to operate and sell.

That evening, Kevin presented the offer to Doctor and Mrs. M. Since the property was in each of their names, Kevin wanted them both present for signatures in case he was successful.

The sellers were very cordial, but told Kevin that they needed the entire down payment of $8,000 in order to purchase another income unit in their new city. They would not be able to hold a note and second mortgage on the property. Kevin spent the next hour considering alternative financing with them to come up with a mutually satisfactory agreement, but without success. In each case, the Simpsons would need all of their Breeding Fund to purchase the property. They wouldn't be using the Power of Leverage.

The Simpsons withdrew their offer.

Activating Your Alternative Plan

The next evening, Kevin and Dianne made an offer on Opportunity C. This opportunity was for a rental home priced at $40,000 with $5,000 down on a real estate contract. The Leverage Ratio at this price was 6.6 to 1.

It needed many Selective Improvements—a few more than the Simpsons wanted to make on their first SFR—but they decided to make an offer for a better price and terms.

They estimated that the unit would need about $3,200 in repairs soon, so they deducted this amount from the seller's asking price of $40,000 and made an offer of $36,800 on a contract with $5,000 down.

The seller of Opportunity C, Bob L., told them he couldn't accept the offer, but would consider a price reduction. Using the See-Saw technique of negotiating described in Chapter 4, the Simpsons made a modified offer of $38,500—just more than halfway between the two figures—if the seller would give them a five year cash-out contract and lower the payments by $25 a month.

Bob agreed and within ten days the buyer and seller had received title insurance, reviewed the real estate contract, signed it and closed the transaction. Kevin and Dianne now owned their first SFR RI and were looking forward to accelerating their equity and doubling their Breeding Fund to $16,000 during WEALTH STAGE 1.

Making Selective Improvements in Your First SFR to Accelerate Equity

Chapter 5 showed you dozens of ways you can build your equity the easy and profitable way by making a few Selective Improvements by:

- Developing low maintenance landscaping
- Installing a low-cost privacy fence
- Painting the exterior of the unit
- Replacing damaged flooring or carpeting
- Painting interior walls
- Remodeling kitchen or bath
- Modernizing heating or lighting

Jack W. made *thousands of dollars* in profits on every rental he purchased by hiring high school students to paint his homes on the weekends. He furnished the paint and lunch at one of the local burger shops. They furnished the labor and he cut his painting costs by more than half.

Not only did Jack save on the cost, but the sprucing up of the home added value to his equity and allowed him to increase rents. Jack made money *three ways* with this one SI technique.

These Investors Build Equity from the First Day

The afternoon their first transaction closed, Kevin and Dianne Simpson were given the keys to their new unit. Notebook in hand, the couple reinspected their investment looking as a renter might to find Selective Improvements that would be valuable to a tenant and profitable for them.

Here's the list they came up with:

- Paint interior of unit
- Modernize kitchen with new sink and linoleum kitchen floor
- Revive and trim lawn

The Simpsons estimated that these three Selective Improvements would cost them about $350 in materials plus their own labor and would increase the value of their unit by over $2,000—well under the SI Rule of spending no more than one-third of the increased value on the Selective Improvement.

Two weeks later the young couple had completed their project and were ready to find their first renter. Of course, during the time they were fixing up the unit, the Simpsons had a sign up in the yard with the new rent: $300 a month—$25 a month more than the previous owner asked. The couple felt that they could easily get that amount with the Selective Improvements that they made on the property since taking it over.

As soon as they were done with their work, Kevin and Dianne placed an ad in the local newspaper:

> FRESHLY DECORATED home near Washington School. Three bedrooms, fireplace, new linoleum in a sunny kitchen. $300 a month plus deposit. 555-4520.

How to Handle Ad Calls and Find the Best Tenants

The calls began soon after the ad appeared. Kevin and Dianne prepared a tenant questionnaire and placed it near the phone to help qualify prospects before time was wasted on both sides. Some of the questions they asked were:

—How many are there in your family?
—Are you renting now? How long have you been there? Could you use your current landlord as a reference?
—Why are you moving?
—Not to be nosey, but to help you qualify for this home, may I ask where you work? How long?
—What is your gross monthly salary?
—Do you have major appliances? Which ones?

USING LEVERAGE IN SFRS

—Do you have any pets? What kind? (If so, explain any pet deposit or fee.)
—When would you like to see the home?

Set up an appointment to show them the unit as soon as possible. In fact, many landlords space appointments about 15 minutes apart so that just about the time the first tenants have seen the unit and stop to decide, the second prospective tenants come in. This shows both groups that the property is in demand and that they should decide right then.

How to Check Out Potential Tenants

From the many people who called and previewed the property, Kevin and Dianne had four prospective tenants that filled out applications to be considered for their rental unit.

Couple A was an older couple on Social Security who hardly qualified for the rent at the current level. Kevin felt that their fixed income would not allow them to bear the eventual rent increases and they would soon have to move.

Couple B were 30 and 32 years of age, had two children that currently attended Washington School. The husband had been on the job at a door factory for seven years, but they had a credit problem and had declared bankruptcy a few years ago.

Couple C was actually two single men who wanted to rent the unit. Their combined incomes were more than enough to qualify them for the rent, but the Simpsons felt that a situation where roommates moved in and out was bad for the landlord because they soon had tenants in their unit that they had not prequalified. They felt that the two men would be better off looking for an apartment.

Couple D had an excellent credit application. They were from out-of-town and it would take over ten days to fully verify their credit through the credit bureau, but after looking over their application, Kevin and Dianne felt that this couple would be the best renters.

Then, on a hunch, Dianne made a few long-distance calls to verify Couple D's application. Each call confirmed the same thing: the application was false. These people were *professional renters* who moved into a unit, then refused to pay rent until they were finally evicted two months to a year later. They moved from city to city living in other people's property rent free.

The Simpsons then reviewed the three remaining couples much as you would on your first SFR. They ruled out Couples A and C and were ready to rule out Couple B because of their credit history when they decided to talk with them more.

Kevin and Dianne met Couple B—LeRoy and Margie T.—at their current home to get an idea of how they kept a house. Though it was a rental, LeRoy and Margie kept their home and yard in good condition. LeRoy seemed to be a handyman and built a workbench and shelves in the garage.

After talking with the couple for about 15 minutes, Dianne asked the potential tenants to explain their bankruptcy and credit problems. Margie volunteered that one of their children, Debbie, had been in the hospital a few times with rheumatic fever and the bills kept them strapped. LeRoy's job now had medical insurance to cover them, but they had to declare medical bankruptcy a few years ago or lose everything they had. Even so, she told them, they had gone back and paid off most of their old creditors since then.

After further discussion, the landlords decided that LeRoy and Margie would make excellent renters. The new tenants agreed to sign a rental agreement and put a deposit down that evening to hold the home until they could get to the bank the following Monday.

Using Productive Marketing to Increase Wealth Stage 1 Profits

The Simpsons's first WEALTH STAGE passed quickly and they were soon ready to cash in the equity in their first RI property. After studying the market carefully, they felt that they could add to their Productive Marketing profit and get a higher price for the unit as a residence rather than as an income property due to the greater demand for residences in their area. They completed a PROPERTY PRICING SHEET which showed that comparable homes were selling for $48,000. They set an asking price of $48,950 and placed an ad in the local newspaper under "Homes For Sale."

Right after they called in the ad, Kevin stopped by to tell their tenants, LeRoy and Margie T., that they were putting the unit on the market and to work out arrangements for showing the property.

That evening, the Simpsons got a call at home. LeRoy said he had just checked with his banker and that they qualified for a 90 percent mortgage with 10 percent down—would they take $48,000 for the home?

Kevin wrote the Purchase and Sale Agreement up that evening and the next day LeRoy and Margie were making application at the bank to purchase the Simpson's rental as their first home.

Five weeks later it was legally theirs.

The Simpsons Reach Their First Wealth Stage Goal

Here's how the Simpsons did financially with the sale of their first SFR:

Original price		$38,500
Equity Gains		
Creative Purchasing		
(purchased below market value)	$ 1,500	
Accelerated Equity—SIs	$ 2,000	
—Appreciation (12%)	$ 5,040	
Productive Marketing (difference)	$ 960	
Total Equity Gains		$ 9,500
Sales Price		$48,000
Less Closing Costs (2%)	$ 960	
Cost of SIs	$ 350	
Mortgage balance	$32,680	
Total Costs and Debts		$33,990
TOTAL EQUITY FROM SFR-1		$14,010
Plus Breeding Fund Balance		$ 2,350
TOTAL EQUITY AND THE END		
OF WEALTH STAGE 1		$16,360

Actually, Kevin and Dianne's profits were higher than this because they had a positive cash flow each month and were able to deduct depreciation of their RI from their income taxes for extra tax savings. Their total is closer to *$18,000,* but the Simpson's experiences and profits illustrate how you can easily build your Breeding Fund to over $16,000 during your first WEALTH STAGE—even if you use techniques in Chapter 3 to start with *little or no capital.*

In practice, you can use the plans and principles outlined in this book to build your Breeding Fund during your first WEALTH STAGE to *$20,000 or more* due to the higher price of SFRs today. In future WEALTH STAGES, profits will actually get *easier* to make because you'll better understand how to apply the advanced techniques of the REAL ESTATE MILLIONAIRE PLAN to increase your equity by 150 percent, 200 percent and more with each transaction.

You can do it—with the REAL ESTATE MILLIONAIRE PLAN.

8

Building Equity in SFRs with High Powered Real Estate Investment Techniques

Congratulations on successfully completing your first WEALTH STAGE and reaching your own financial goal. You've used the steps and techniques of the REAL ESTATE MILLIONAIRE PLAN to purchase your first Single Family Residence Residential Income property, then operate and sell it at a substantial profit. You've successfully applied the REMAP System.

If you're following the suggested goal of making your first quarter million in real estate in five WEALTH STAGES or years, you now have an investment equity of *over* $16,000. And your goal during WEALTH STAGE 2 is to *double your equity* to $32,000.

You'll find it much easier to reach this goal because you now have experience in actually finding Property with Potential, using the Power of Leverage and Imaginative Financing, taking advantage of Creative Purchasing techniques to buy profitable RIs, building Accelerated Equity with Selective Improvements, and understanding how to add *extra profits* to your bank account with Productive Marketing.

Whatever your WEALTH STAGE 2 goal is, you'll be able to

expand your profits with these advanced methods of using the REAL ESTATE MILLIONAIRE PLAN.

Finding More Properties with Potential for Earning Substantial Profits

Before you move to WEALTH STAGE 2, let's look back over the successes and near-successes of your first WEALTH STAGE.

- Did you use the Power of Leverage to increase your profits with a high Leverage Ratio?
- Did you profit from Creative Purchasing by finding a highly motivated seller?
- Were you able to take advantage of many Selective Improvements and accelerate your equity?
- Did you make Productive Marketing work for you and earn extra profits by selling your SFR on the best price and terms?
- Did you reach your WEALTH STAGE goal?

Floyd E. reviewed his first WEALTH STAGE—a two year period with a goal of $20,000—with satisfaction. He started with a Breeding Fund of less than $1,000 and was able to purchase two older homes on the same block from an investor who wanted to retire. Using the incentive of a full-price offer, Floyd was able to get both homes with excellent terms—no down payment and two months before the first payment was due.

Floyd used the two months to make a few Selective Improvements and get renters in the units. By making small SIs during the two years, he was able to increase the rents from $220 to $295 a month each—and bring their market value up from $33,000 to $44,500 each.

Looking back on his first WEALTH STAGE, Floyd saw that he more than reached his $20,000-two-year goal, but that he could have made an even greater profit by—

- Purchasing more units from the same retiring seller

BUILDING EQUITY IN SFRS

- Using Productive Marketing techniques to get a better price when he sold his units
- Using Creative Purchasing methods to buy the units at a lower price

Floyd E. promised himself that he would improve the near-successes he had during WEALTH STAGE 1 and make even more than the *$50,000 goal* he had set for WEALTH STAGE 2.

How These Smart Investors Learned Profit Secrets by Reviewing Wealth Stage 1

Kevin and Dianne Simpson did the same thing—they decided to review their first WEALTH STAGE and profit from it.

The Simpsons purchased SFR-1 with $5,000 on a $38,500 price tag. Their $5,300 bred $33,500 in Rented Money for a Leverage Ratio of 6.6 to 1. They felt that this was fairly good for their first unit, but wanted to improve on this ratio for even higher profits during WEALTH STAGE 2.

SFR-1 had a number of Selective Improvements, but the Simpsons only took advantage of a few of them. Even so, they earned $1,650 in clear, easy profits with SIs. Now they realized that they could handle even more Selective Improvements profitably.

They purchased SFR-1 with Imaginative Financing—a real estate contract. In WEALTH STAGE 2 they wanted to try other IF techniques to increase their Power of Leverage.

Finally, Kevin and Dianne analyzed that they had earned a price reduction of $1,500 when they purchased SFR-1 with Creative Purchasing techniques, but they felt that having a third party negotiate for them might be even more profitable. In their study of local SFRs, the Simpsons ran across the name of one Realtor who seemed to specialize in working with small investors: Don C. Remembering that the sales commission is paid by the seller and that the Realtor's fee is not charged to the buyer, Kevin and Dianne called Don at Aztec Realty and set up an appointment to see if they could work together.

After meeting Don, the Simpsons felt confident that he could help them reach their goals more easily and asked him to look for two or three SFRs to purchase as Residential Income properties with the proceeds from the sale of SFR-1.

How Don C. Found Five Properties with Potential

The Simpsons were looking for motivated sellers. They realized that a seller who needed to move his units quickly because of financial or health reasons would be more interested in accepting a lower offer or better terms.

You can find a highly motivated seller by checking these places:

- *Local Courthouse:* Hundreds of smart RI investors find all of their best buys by checking courthouse records. They check the tax department for delinquent owners who may be soon be forced to sell. They check the county clerk's office for divorce and estate filings.

- *Financial Institutions:* Other sharp investors work primarily with savings and loan associations, mutual banks, mortgage companies, FHA and VA offices to assume foreclosures and repossessions.

- *Offers to buy:* Still other REMAP investors keep an ad in their local paper offering to buy homes and income property for cash knowing that those who call on such ads are highly motivated.

That's what the Simpsons asked Don to look for—highly motivated sellers.

Don set the first Home Search appointment with them for the following Saturday morning. He had five units for them to inspect and when he picked them up at their home he gave them notepads so they could discuss each unit later.

Inspecting SFRs for Profitability

Opportunity D was a three bedroom home currently a residence for a young couple. It was their first home. The husband was being transferred to a better job in a neighboring state and had to move. Their price was $42,000 cash. Don explained that the couple needed all of their equity in cash to make the move and purchase a home in their new town. They were motivated to sell. An inspection of the property showed the Simpsons that there were many SIs that could be made to increase the value of this property in just a few weeks.

Opportunity E was another owner-occupied home that the Realtor felt might be a potential rental unit. Kevin and Dianne saw few Selective Improvements available and felt that the neighborhood was too good for the type of rental they were searching for. Don explained that the seller was not as motivated and was only putting his home on the market in hopes of getting a high price and moving to something larger. His price reflected the low motivation: $49,000. Don showed it to them as a comparison.

Opportunity F was priced at $41,000 and as soon as the couple stepped in they could see why it was priced low. It had been a rental for over ten years and was in disrepair. Don said that the seller had accepted an offer of $39,000 earlier, but that the buyers didn't qualify and the home was back on the market. Don felt that they could pick up the home for $39,000 *or less* depending on terms. The Simpsons wanted profitable SIs, but felt this unit would need some unprofitable repairs first.

Opportunity G was actually *Opportunities G* and *H*. It was two SFR rentals owned by the same man. He bought them new five years earlier and had depreciated them to the point where they were no longer offering him the tax shelter he wanted. There was also too much cash flow. His mortgage payments—set five years ago—were much lower than his current rents and he had a high positive cash flow. As an investor he wanted a low positive cash flow and decided to sell the units. They were priced at $45,000 each. The mortgages, with balances of $27,000, were nonassumable, which meant that a buyer would either have to come up with the $18,000 difference per home or refinance. The seller said he was willing to take a second mortgage back on the properties.

On inspecting Opportunities G and H, Kevin commented that there were many Selective Improvements that could make these units profitable. They surmised that the seller had purchased the units, then forgot them. They showed heavy wear, but there was nothing structurally wrong with them.

Making a Decision on the Best SFRs

When they returned to the Realtor's office, Kevin and Dianne asked Don to give them figures on how close to market value these units were and what investment benefits they would earn with each opportunity. Don had previously done a COMPARATIVE MARKET ANALYSIS and an INVESTMENT ANALYSIS—similar to the PROPERTY PRICING SHEET and INCOME PROPERTY ANALYSIS you've seen in this book—for each of the five units.

After looking them over, Kevin, Dianne and Don spread out all the facts before them to narrow the five opportunities down to two or three.

Looking back over their successes and problems with SFR-1, the Simpsons decided to eliminate Opportunity E because the unit was obviously overpriced at $49,000 and the seller didn't seem motivated to lower the price at all. They were sure that the seller would not sell his unit until he reduced his price by at least $4,000.

Reviewing their notes, Opportunity D looked good to the Simpsons. The seller was motivated and might even take a reduced offer before he had to move to his new job out-of-state. He wanted cash, but they knew they could get a conventional loan to give the seller cash if they wanted the unit.

Opportunity F was not as good because it needed many repairs. The Simpsons marked this one "maybe."

They all agreed that Opportunities G and H sounded the most profitable if they could find some way to finance them. They decided to make an offer on them if they could get some Imaginative Financing.

BUILDING EQUITY IN SFRS

Making Imaginative Financing Work for You with a Creative Wrap-Around Mortgage

Wrap-arounds are one of the most creative—and most misunderstood—methods of financing RI property. I'm going to show you how you can open up hundreds of new financial opportunities for yourself by using the safe and profitable *Wrap-Around*.

Actually, the Wrap-Around mortgage is nothing more than a second mortgage. It works like this: rather than paying the seller off with the proceeds of a conventional loan, the buyer makes payments directly to the seller. The seller then takes part of your payment and continues to make payments on the property's original loan. The rest of your payment is his as a second mortgage.

George A. sold his SFR to Marilyn R. on a wrap-around. The purchase price was $52,000. Marilyn paid George 10 percent down—$5,200—and the balance of $46,800 at 9½ percent interest with payments of $393.53 a month. George still owed $29,000 on the property with payments of $212.80 at 8 percent interest.

Rather than pay this first mortgage off, George took a second mortgage position on the property—second in line in case of default—and was able to keep the proceeds. He got the down payment, kept the difference in monthly payments of $180.73—plus was able to make an extra 1½ percent interest each month on the first mortgage. Most important, in case of default he was in the best position to take the property back and resell it at an even bigger profit.

The advantage to the buyer is that she was able to purchase the unit with only 10 percent down and less credit problems.

Smart RI investors use Wrap-Arounds whenever they can in buying and selling property.

Kevin and Dianne Use a Wrap-Around to Creatively Purchase Two Profitable Units

The Simpson's Realtor, Don, presented the offer to the owner of Opportunities G and H. It went like this:

> Price: $80,000 for both units
> Terms: $8,000 down and a Wrap-Around mortgage with payments of $600 a month at 9½ percent interest, cash-out in four years or less.

Don showed the seller, Mike T., how he would benefit from this wrap-around.

	PRICE	TERMS
SALE PRICE	$80,000	$600/mo.
FIRST MORTGAGE	$54,000	$396.25 (8%)
PROFIT	$26,000	$203.75

In other words, Mike would profit $26,000 with the down payment of $8,000 in cash (less sales and closing costs) and the balance at *over $200 a month for 30 years.*

Mike signed.

Kevin pulled out his calculator and figured the Leverage Ratio: $72,000 Rented Money divided by $8,000 investment equals a Leverage Ratio of 9—nearly half-again better than the ratio of SFR-1.

How to Use Preapproved Financing and Buy like Cash

The seller doesn't care where you get the money to cash him out as long as it's *legal tender*. Here's how one sharp RI investor made sellers an *all-cash offer* for a *reduced price*.

Ben H. had bought and sold SFRs for more than six years, making a profit on every one, before he accidentally discovered this technique. One day at lunch his banker told him he would probably qualify for any loan on any rental he wanted to buy under $50,000. Ben started thinking. If he had preapproved financing before he ever made an offer on a home, he was actually an all-cash buyer—a very rare bird.

Ben tried this idea out on his opportunity. He found a unit that looked profitable, especially if it could be picked up at a good price. The seller was very motivated and needed cash to clear up some past bills or lose his car, furniture and credit. Ben made the seller a cash offer $6,000 *under* his asking price and told him the offer was good for ten days. The seller turned it down, but on the tenth day he called Ben and told him he'd accept it.

Two weeks later the seller had his cash and Ben had a Golden Opportunity.

BUILDING EQUITY IN SFRS

All you have to do to get prearranged financing is talk with your banker about the type of unit you're looking for, tell him how much down you'll be putting on it and give him some financial history. If you have good credit, you may qualify for a mortgage before you find the right unit and be able to buy like cash.

These Investors Made $5,000 with Imaginative Financing

Don, the Simpson's Realtor, told them about the Imaginative Financing technique you just learned about—Prearranged Financing—and decided to put it to work with an offer on Opportunity D.

As you remember, the sellers of Opportunity D were moving to a neighboring state and were asking $42,000 for their home. The Simpsons decided to make them an all-cash offer of $37,000 through Don.

"We just can't accept anything less than $40,000 on our house," the sellers told him.

"Have you had *any* offers?"

"Well, just one ridiculous one of $35,000—but we didn't accept it."

"If you had to move to your new job tomorrow or face losing it, would you accept that $35,000 offer today?" Don asked.

"Well," said the seller, "I suppose we'd *have* to."

"The offer I have for you today is $2,000 *more* than the lowest offer you'll accept—and it's *all cash.* Can you live with that offer?"

They could and within two weeks they were on their way to the new job with the proceeds in cash. And the Simpsons now had a third SFR.

How to Multiply Profits with a Gross Rent Multiplier

Here's another advanced Accelerated Equity technique you can use to set the *best rent* and put the *right price* on an SFR. It's called the *Gross Rent Multiplier* method. It offers a factor or ratio of fair market value to fair market rent. Here's an example.

GROSS RENT MULTIPLIER

SFR VALUE:	$48,000	RENT:	$320 mo.	GRM: 150
SFR VALUE:	$41,500	RENT:	$275 mo.	GRM: 151
SFR VALUE:	$43,000	RENT:	$280 mo.	GRM: 154
SFR VALUE:	$44,000	RENT:	$300 mo.	GRM: 147

AVERAGE SFR GROSS RENT MULTIPLIER IN THIS AREA 150

In other words, typical rents in this area could be found by dividing the market value by 150. This method of finding the typical rents based on the market value can be used in any part of the country. The GRM in your area might be 130 or 162 or 125. In each case, the Gross Rent Multiplier can easily be found using the method above.

Putting Your GRM into Action

Kevin and Dianne Simpson used a Gross Rent Multiplier to decide on the rents they would charge for their new units—SFR-2, -3 and -4.

Since Opportunities G and H were renting for $300 a month, the GRM would indicate a value of 45,000 each—exactly what the seller originally asked for the units. Opportunity D had not been a rental, but they found that a comparable unit would rent for $275, so the GRM would indicate a market value of $41,250.

These figures meant that on the day the Simpsons purchased their three SFRs they made *$14,250 in equity* by buying the units at below the indicated GRM value—thanks to Don and Creative Purchasing.

The Simpsons planned on making even more money with Selective Improvements that would raise the rent on Opportunity D from $275 to $300 a month and Opportunities G and H from $300 to $325 a month—an increase of $3,750 per unit ($25 × 150 GRM) if they could improve the units enough to justify a $25 a month rent increase.

How to Turn Quick Dollars with Easy SIs

The easiest—and most profitable—Selective Improvements a smart investor can make are the ones that improve the looks of the unit with little cost. These *cosmetic* SIs have made *millions of dollars* for the hundreds of RI investors who have caught onto them.

One of those wealthy investors, Barry P., has made over $50,000 in *extra profits* during the past six years with just one of these cosmetic SIs: landscaping. He's always enjoyed working in the yard, so when he bought his first Single Family Residence rental, he naturally decided that the yard was the first thing he would fix up.

The edges of the lawn were very rough, but the center seemed to be healthy, so Barry spent a weekend cutting a three foot wide border around the lawn. He then filled the area with bark dust and gravel, added a few easy care plants, threw some lawn food on the grass and stood back. For a cost of about $150, Barry was able to get $15 more a month in rent. Using a GRM of 150, that's an increase in value of about $2,250.

Soon, Barry was buying up units that especially needed landscaping and light cosmetics for 10 to 20 percent *below* market value. With cosmetic SIs he was profiting $3,000 to $12,000 on every unit.

Today, Barry spends much of his time in his own Japanese Garden attached to his $200,000 home in southern California—all because he majored in cosmetics.

The Simpsons Turn Cosmetics into Cash

After taking title to their three new RIs, Kevin and Dianne made their first tours of the properties in order to decide on the most profitable Selective Improvements.

Opportunities G and H—which they now called SFR-2 and -3—were nearly identical and, with few exceptions, took the same Selective Improvements. After five years of low maintenance both units needed:

- Carpeting in the living rooms and hallways
- Repainting inside walls and ceilings
- Replace one door

By shopping around they found a supplier for the carpet who would replace the carpet throughout both units for the same price other suppliers wanted to charge for just the living room and hallways. After checking their Breeding Fund balance, Kevin and Dianne decided to have them do it.

The couple then decided that, to save money, they would paint the interiors themselves before the new carpet was installed. In fact, since the old carpet was going to be pulled up soon, they decided not to use drop cloths. They rented a spray painter for a day and in one weekend they added thousands of dollars in value to SFR-2 and -3 with cosmetic SIs.

SFR-4—which was originally Opportunity D—needed more modernizing than cleaning up. Their SI list for SFR-4 read:

- Refinish kitchen cabinets and replace handles
- Replace linoleum in kitchen and bath
- Replace bathroom sink with modern cabinet and sink
- Wallpaper bathroom
- Install Franklin fireplace with brick base

Total cost: $500 plus labor.

Using Accelerated Equity techniques, the Simpsons soon had profitable renters in all three of their new SFRs—at higher rents.

Cashing in on Accelerated Equity

To turn your Accelerated Equity into Substantial Profits, you need to use the advanced techniques of Productive Marketing—getting the best price and terms.

The Simpsons second WEALTH STAGE passed quickly and soon it was time to use Productive Marketing again. To stay on schedule with their REAL ESTATE MILLIONAIRE PLAN and the WEALTH STAGES they set up, Kevin and Dianne had to decide how they were going to pull their Accelerated Equity from their three RIs and move on to WEALTH STAGE 3.

They knew that their options were to—

- Sell
- Refinance

They also knew *Ramsey's Rule of Productive Marketing*:

Never sell a winner!

Since they had made the Selective Improvements to SFR-4—the one with the fireplace and modernization—they had little trouble renting it and knew that it would command a much higher rent than they were asking when they first improved it. For this and other reasons they decided on hang on to SFR-4 and refinance it.

The two identical units—SFR-2 and -3—were good rental units, but Kevin felt that they were not as profitable as they were a year ago. Their value was at the high end of the rental market for that type of unit and they had developed nearly all of the Selective Improvements they could from them. Since the year's appreciation had brought the current rents to $350 a month, their value was estimated at $52,500 each.

How Two Investors Refinanced for Quick Cash

By developing a PROPERTY PRICING SHEET, the Simpsons discovered that appreciation and other Accelerated Equity methods had increased the fair market value of SFR-4 to $49,950 and that it should be renting for about $333 a month ($49,950 ÷ 150 GRM). Checking comparable rentals, they decided that the rent on this unit could be increased to $330 a month and still be competitive.

The banker that helped them purchase SFR-4 a year earlier was willing to refinance it at 80 percent of its current market value, or $39,960. The monthly payments would be $336 which would give the Simpsons a slight negative cash flow, but would allow them to pull most of their Accelerated Equity out while still keeping the unit as a growing rental.

Let's take a look at the profit statement from the refinancing of SFR-4:

Original Price	$37,000
Equity Gains	
Creative Purchasing	$ 4,250
Accelerated Equity—Selective Imp.	$ 3,750
—Appreciation	$ 4,950
Productive Marketing	$ -0-
Total Equity Gains	$12,950
Current Value	$49,950
Less Down Payment	$ 7,400
Closing costs (on purchase)	$ 1,200
Mortgage balance	$29,000
Cost of Selective Improvements	$ 1,300
Refinance costs (1% loan fee)	$ 400
Total Costs	$39,300
TOTAL PROFIT FROM SFR-4	$10,650

The refinancing of SFR-4 gave the Simpsons a lump sum of $8,060 in cash while still leaving an equity of 20 percent, or $9,990, in SFR-4. If needed, they could always borrow more against their remaining equity. In the meantime, they had over $8,000 in anticipation of WEALTH STAGE 3.

How the Simpsons Made Big Profits Selling SFR-2 and -3

Kevin and Dianne decided to sell their other two units to families rather than investors because home buyers were less likely to attempt to make a drastically cut offer. Based on what similar homes were selling for in their area, they listed the units with Don, their Realtor, at $54,950 each.

Within two weeks Don brought them an acceptable offer on each unit: $54,500 on SFR-2 and $54,950 with two points FHA on SFR-3. They actually netted more on SFR-2 because the FHA offer required that they pay two points, or 2 percent—$1,099—to help the purchaser with his loan.

Here's how the Simpsons made out on the sales of SFR-2 and -3:

BUILDING EQUITY IN SFRS

Original Price		$80,000
Equity Gains		
Creative Purchasing	$10,000	
Accelerated Equity—Selective Imp.	$ 7,500	
—Appreciation	$10,800	
Productive Marketing (difference)	$ 1,150	
Total Equity Gains		$29,450
Sales Price		$109,450
Less Closing costs (original purchase)	$ 800	
Down Payment	$ 8,000	
Mortgage balance	$69,800	
Cost of Selective Improvements	$ 2,250	
Closing costs (with FHA points)	$ 6,035	
Sales commissions (6%)	$ 6,567	
Total Costs		$93,452
TOTAL PROFIT FROM SFR-2 AND -3		**$15,998**

Now let's recap the Simpson's wealth at the end of WEALTH STAGE 2:

Equity at the beginning of WEALTH STAGE 2	$16,360
Profit from refinance of SFR-4	$10,650
Profit from sale of SFR-2 and -3	$15,998
TOTAL EQUITY AT THE END OF WEALTH STAGE 2	$43,008

This total, of course, is before taxes, but with the component depreciation and interest payment credits that the Simpsons were able to take advantage of they had a *tax shelter* and didn't have to pay taxes on any of this profit.

Their financial goal for WEALTH STAGE 2 was only $32,000—and they passed it by over 34 percent. Why? For many reasons, but basically because they were able to use many Accelerated Equity techniques to make their equity grow in each investment they owned. Also Don, their Realtor, was able to earn them $14,250 in CP profits while his commissions were only $6,567, so he made them over $7,600 in clear profits.

They also earned profits through a high rate of appreciation. Even though the national average for appreciation on all types of real estate was closer to 10 percent a year, Kevin and Dianne knew how to choose units in growth areas where appreciation was 12 *percent and more* each year.

Of course, much of their extra profits came from their willingness to "take a risk" and move from one SFR to three SFRs. Even though they used the REAL ESTATE MILLIONAIRE PLAN to guarantee themselves against loss, the extra "risk" paid them back handsomely.

WEALTH STAGE 2 is over for the Simpsons. They are now holding over $43,000 in cash and equity—*one-third* over their goal—and they're anxiously looking forward to WEALTH STAGE 3.

You should be, too.

9

Switching to MFDs to Increase Income and Lower Expenses

If you're following my suggested WEALTH STAGES, you're well on your way to making your first *quarter million dollars* in real estate in five years. You've learned how to apply the REAL ESTATE MILLIONAIRE PLAN profitably and double your equity each year for two years. You have built your Breeding Fund into more than $32,000. Fantastic!

Now let's double your goal again—and set it for $64,000 in the next twelve months of WEALTH STAGE 3. The method is simple: take your profits from Single Family Residences—SFRs—and invest it in higher-profit Multi-Family Dwellings—or MFDs.

But whatever your goal during WEALTH STAGE 3, you can easily reach it with the investment techniques you'll learn about in the coming pages.

Let's get going.

MFDs—The Most Profitable RI Properties

Just what is a Multi-Family Dwelling? It's a building or group of buildings expressly designed to house more than one family. An

SFR is designed for just one family either as a primary residence for its owners *or* as a rental investment property. An MFD is a pure Residential Income property and normally isn't sold as a residence. It's sold as a source of income and appreciation for its buyers.

There are many kinds of Multi-Family Dwellings, but they can be broken down into two main categories by the number of units in each:

- PLEXES: Duplexes, triplexes and fourplexes with either two, three or four rental units in one building.
- APARTMENTS: Groupings of five or more RI units in one building or close grouping of buildings. This can be a 12-unit apartment complex or three fourplexes grouped together.

Though many MFD investors start with Plexes and work up to Apartment ownership, this book suggests you move right from SFRs to Apartment MFDs. Why? Because Plexes aren't much different than SFRs. The management problems are about the same as apartments and the return on your investment isn't much more than SFRs. You've worked with SFRs for two years now and you've earned the right to move up to the more profitable field of Multi-Family Dwellings.

MFDs make a better investment for the experienced RI investor for many reasons:

- Higher income per investment dollar
- Lower expenses per investment dollar
- Better cash flow than SFRs
- Better tax shelter than SFRs
- Risks are higher, but more controlled
- Equity growth is quicker

Higher Income

Because MFDs are primarily a Residential Income property and usually not sold to people other than investors, they go by a different set of rules than the SFR that has value to both the investor and the home buyer. MFDs have slightly higher risk and less liquidity than SFRs, but they make up for it by offering a better income for the number of investment dollars you put into them. MFDs are also more income- and cost-conscious than SFRs. In other words, units are built with cost-per-dollar-returned in mind. Floor plans are more economical and there's usually little wasted space in an MFD. They are basic units that are built at a specific cost to earn a specific rent and return a specific amount of income. Their efficiency brings you a higher return per dollar.

For example, Dudley N. purchased his first MFD—a six-unit apartment complex—for $120,000. His monthly income was $1,200 (6 times $200). For the same $120,000 he could have purchased only three $40,000 homes renting for about $265 a month each for an income of $795 a month. That's about two-thirds as much income for the same total investment dollars.

MFDs Offer Lower Expenses

This investment efficiency carries over to the expenses. An MFD requires less maintenance, yardwork and other costs. The costs of management, maintenance and vacancies are less in MFDs because the units are all in one location. Management can control the units better and watch for vandalism or damage more easily.

Lyle A. traded his six SFRs in for a 12-unit complex in his town. In doing so, he not only began earning a higher income each month, but he cut his expenses down by being able to keep a better eye on his investment. His half-dozen SFRs were spread out in a six mile circle. He had to make special trips to each unit to collect rents, do maintenance, check for damages and talk with tenants. With his new MFD he had just one location to watch and he was able to share losses between more units. Lyle cut his overhead and raised his income by trading in his SFRs for MFDs.

Better Cash Flow

MFDs also offer a better cash flow than SFRs. MFDs are RI properties and owners expect a higher positive cash flow—more income than expenses—than they do with SFRs. The REAL ESTATE MILLIONAIRE PLAN discourages a heavy cash flow in order to earn higher leverage and appreciation, but when you sell your MFD a positive cash flow will entice many buyers looking for income over equity build-up.

Tax Shelter

MFDs give you a better tax shelter than SFRs. This shelter is earned because you're no longer depreciating a $40,000 house—your're depreciating a $150,000 to $250,000 apartment complex. The straight line depreciation on a $250,000 complex for 40 years is $6,250 *each year*. That's $6,250 of income you won't have to pay taxes on.

Controlled Risks

Another reason why MFDs are your next logical step is *risk*. More units and a larger total investment naturally mean more risk. But the two year education you've received with SFRs will qualify you as a knowledgeable investor who can easily reduce this risk to a minimum. The fact that your units are all in one location will also help you minimize risk.

Steve B. cut risks when he switched from SFRs to MFDs because he moved into one of his apartment units and served as manager. Not only was he able to keep damages and risk down, but he also qualified for a better loan from his mortgage company because the unit was "owner occupied."

Equity Growth

Finally, MFDs offer you something that SFRs did, but on a larger scale: growth. After all, would you rather be earning a 12 percent a year appreciation on a $45,000 SFR or a $225,000 MFD? Multi-Family Dwellings offer you more growth with Selective Improvements, Equity Build-up and other Accelerated Equity techniques because you're working with RIs that are worth more. The Power of Leverage also works better on MFDs.

In fact, you'll find dozens of ways to build your fortune and reach your personal wealth goal by applying the REAL ESTATE MILLIONAIRE PLAN to Multi-Family Dwellings.

The Smartest Investors Use This Formula

By now you're ready to use one of the greatest tools offered to the smart real estate investor: the *Capitalization Rate* or Cap Rate. The Cap Rate is the rate that an investment pays you back each year. It's used by the biggest and the smartest investors in the world. Here's how it works.

Let's say you have $1,000 in cash and that you put it in a bank paying 7 percent interest per annum. You put it in on January 1 and can expect to have $1,070 on December 31. Well, real estate investing is supposedly riskier than banks so you'd probably want a better return on your money. Let's say you'd like to earn 12 percent on your money. That is, $1,000 on January 1 would be worth $1,120 on December 31. Much better—especially when you consider that you're making 12 percent on the *entire value* of the property, not just on your investment in it. That is, if you have a $10,000 equity in a $200,000 property and you earn a 12 percent return—a Cap Rate of 12 percent—you are earning $24,000 a year. That's 12 percent of the $200,000. Actually, you're earning a *240 percent return* on your original $10,000 investment. And that's how real estate millionaires are made.

Cap Rates and Rent

You can also use Capitalization Rates to set the rents on your property. If your $200,000 property is two fourplexes, you can figure what you must get out of each unit per month like this:

PRICE	×	CAP RATE	÷	UNITS	÷	MONTHS	=	RENT
$200,000	×	12%	÷	8	÷	12	=	$250

In other words, each of your eight units must rent for $250 a month in order to give you a return or Cap Rate of 12 percent a year. This rental charge should be confirmed by comparing rents of similar units in your area to make sure that renters are willing to pay $250 a month for your units. If so, you can earn 12 percent per year on the entire value of your property.

You can also use the Cap Rate to show potential buyers how

you justify your sales price when you decide to cash in your equity. The Cap Rate can be your best friend in helping you decide whether an MFD will be profitable and where you need to set your rents for a good return on your dollar.

Back to the ballgame. Let's learn how to check MFDs for profitability.

How to Find an MFD Property with Potential

Before you go on your first tour of profitable MFDs in search for the best buy, let's review and modify the methods of inspecting Residential Income properties to ensure you have all the facts when you make your decision.

Smart MFD investors will inspect Properties with Potential for these things:

- *History of Property*—How old is this MFD? Who built it? When? Who has owned it since then? Has it always been a profitable unit?

- *Inspection of Property*—What condition are the units in? Can you inspect each of them before making an offer "Subject to satisfactory inspection"? Are all the units in the same condition? What profitable Selective Improvements could you make? Are there any unprofitable repairs that must be made soon? What appliances or personal property are included in the sale? Have you verified the inventory?

- *Inspection of Records*—Are the owner's books up-to-date? Is he making a profit? How much? What are his vacancy and management percentages? Are they realistic? When were the rents last increased?

- *Motivation of Seller*—How motivated is the seller? Why is he selling? Will he accept a lower price? Better terms? Can his current mortgage be assumed? When does he want to transfer title?

SWITCHING TO MFDS

As you can see, REMAP STEP 1—finding Property with Potential—that you successfully applied to SFRs can easily be applied to MFDs with only a few changes.

Let's see how our model investors found their first MFD Property with Potential.

Searching for Your First Profitable MFD

To show you exactly how you can build your fortune with the REAL ESTATE MILLIONAIRE PLAN, we've been following one couple through their five WEALTH STAGES. Whether your own personal goal and WEALTH STAGES are the same or vastly different from Kevin and Dianne Simpson's, you can learn many advanced investment techniques by watching them successfully apply REMAP.

The first MFD they inspected—which we'll call *Opportunity I*—was a 12-unit converted motel. It was in fair condition, about 35 years old, with the conversion done about ten years ago. The units were one bedroom apartments that rented for $200 a month due to its proximity to the industrial area. Inspection of the MFD indicated that the remodeling was shoddy and that even though it had been done just ten years ago, the MFD showed its full age of 35 years. The Simpsons also felt that, though the unit was near the industrial park and would attract many long-term workers as renters, they would prefer a complex nearer a residential area that had two bedroom units to encourage small families rather than singles to rent from them.

Opportunity J was a fourplex in excellent condition. It was only six months old and was priced at $100,000. The four units rented for $275 each per month. After inspecting the property, Kevin and Dianne agreed that they might consider such a small complex if the rents were competitive. They applied their Cap Rate formula to the property using 12 percent and came up with a projected rent of $250 a month per unit based on the purchase price. Though $275 a month would give them a better return on their investment, they felt that the rent was above the fair market rent for the units.

Opportunity K was a remodeled eight-unit apartment complex near the downtown area. It was priced at $175,000. Rents were $200 a month and four of them—half of the total—were vacant.

The Simpson's inspection told them why: a poor manager kept the building littered with trash and hadn't painted the interior or exterior of the building in seven years. All painting—which was negligible—had been done by the tenants. Kevin checked the structure itself and felt that it was sound, but needed a lot of minor work to make it profitable. This was tempting, but Kevin and Dianne weren't sure they wanted to take on the task of fixing up this rundown complex—profit or not.

They thought it over. By applying their Cap Rate of 12 percent to the current rent schedule *if* it were fully rented, they came up with a sale price of $160,000. They knew that if they were to purchase it for more than that they wouldn't get a 12 percent return on their investment. They had to make a decision.

Reconsidering the Opportunities

The Simpsons looked at Opportunities I and J again. They felt that it would take too many unprofitable repairs to make Opportunity I a good investment. The price and rents fit their Cap Rate, but they decided against an offer because the repairs would take too much of their capital and lower their Power of Leverage.

Opportunity J's rents were too high. For that reason, and because the fourplex was not large enough to build their fortune with, they decided against it, too.

Kevin and Dianne finally decided that if they could purchase Opportunity K—the eight unit apartment complex—at or below $160,000, they would take it.

How Imaginative Financing Can Turn the Key on Your First MFD

Bankers are as interested in Capitalization Rates as you are.

Tucker, Incorporated, a real estate investment group composed of businessmen from a small New Mexico town, used their Cap Rate to get them a loan on a highly profitable MFD in their town.

Their opportunity was a 24-unit apartment complex that was

listed at $500,000. The units were currently renting for $245 each with a vacancy factor of just 1 percent. Tucker, Incorporated, needed financing to buy it. They took all their figures to their bank. The banker seemed unable to help them until one of the partners pointed out to the loan officer that the Capitalization Rate on this property was *14 percent*—the investors were earning a return of over 14 percent per year on the total investment. He further showed the bank that the corporation was putting $50,000 of its own money into the investment and would actually be earning a return of *140 percent per year*.

With this information the partnership not only got the loan they wanted, but they also got a new partner in the corporation—the bank president—who could virtually assure them loans on future investments.

They used their Cap Rate to both check the profitability of their venture and ensure the repayment of the loan to a bank.

Smart Money Techniques for Negotiating a Creative Purchase

You've come a long way in understanding and applying the REAL ESTATE MILLIONAIRE PLAN. By now you're ready to use these advanced Creative Purchasing techniques to earn even higher profits with MFDs:

- Draw up a projected net cash flow on the MFD once you buy it. If you're using high leverage you'll have a smaller positive cash flow than the current owner. Use this fact to let the seller or broker know you won't make much profit from cash flow and that price and terms are more important to you.

- Stress the disadvantages of the purchase. The seller is going to fill you in on every advantage he can think of while you're considering the property. Stress that the purchase is risky, that you will only buy it if you can do so profitably, that there is a great deal of maintenance and repairs to be done (if so) and that your Property Pricing Sheet shows that it's priced above market value. By stressing the negative side of the purchase, you are balancing the seller's optimism.

- Increase your Power of Leverage by putting no more than 10 percent down on the property. Give a note and second mortgage back to the seller, ask the real estate broker to take a note for some or all of his commission, sell a second mortgage to a mortgage broker or private lender.

- Check Excise Tax or Revenue Stamps paid when the seller purchased the property. In nearly every state the government requires the seller to pay either an excise tax or recording tax that is in direct proportion to the final sales price. You can use the seller's purchase price to show him how much he has made on the property.

Doug and Marty F. purchased their first MFD by using this Creative Purchasing technique. The six-unit apartment complex they were looking at was listed at $150,000. Rents were $250 a month per unit.

Marty pulled a Customer Service Package on the units from his title company. It showed that the seller purchased the complex four years earlier for an undisclosed amount. The recorded document in the courthouse did show that the seller paid $900 in excise tax on the sale. Marty was told by the courthouse that his state required a 1 percent excise tax be paid on all property sold in it. Simple math told Marty that the sale price was evidently $90,000.

Marty further computed that with an appreciation rate of 12 percent a year, the current value should actually be about $135,000—not the $150,000 the seller was asking.

With these facts, Doug and Marty were able to persuade the owner to sell the sixplex to them for $135,000. They saved $15,000 with this one Creative Purchasing technique.

Using Advanced Creative Purchasing Techniques to Negotiate a Profitable Transaction

Kevin Simpson had learned a great deal about negotiating by the time he was ready to present the offer on his first MFD. He knew not to purchase any unit that couldn't make him a healthy profit. He also knew that smart negotiators ask the seller for a few concessions that they will later relinquish to the seller to help him save face.

Here's the offer the Simpsons made on Opportunity K, the eight-unit apartment complex priced at $175,000.

> PURCHASER AGREES TO PAY $150,000 WITH $135,000 IN CASH AT CLOSING AND THE SELLER TO TAKE A NOTE AND SECOND MORTGAGE FOR THE BALANCE OF $15,000 WITH INTEREST-ONLY PAYMENTS ANNUALLY AND PRINCIPAL DUE IN FIVE YEARS.

Using the See-Saw technique of negotiating introduced in Chapter 4, Kevin traded these concessions:

- Upped purchase price to $160,000
- Two year cash-out on second mortgage

for these concessions from the seller:

- Second mortgage upped to $22,000
- $2,400 credit toward vacancies

Since Kevin expected to pay $160,000 for the property and planned on making his profit and selling it within two years anyway, his concessions weren't hard to make. For them, he was able to purchase a $160,000 MFD with an 80 percent conventional loan from a mortgage broker and just $7,600 *of his own cash*. This is a Leverage Ratio of over 21 to 1—his best yet.

Kevin's advanced negotiating techniques made the difference.

The transaction was signed and closed within 30 days and the Simpsons had made another successful purchase with the REAL ESTATE MILLIONAIRE PLAN.

Setting a GRM for Your MFD

The last chapter introduced you to the surest way to set rents and quickly decide on market value: the *Gross Rent Multiplier*. The GRM is the ratio of fair market value to fair market rent in your area. Let's see how this magical multiplier can be used on MFDs.

Cherie D. was ready to purchase her first Multi-Family Dwelling when she discovered Gross Rent Multipliers. Using information from the "For Rent" column of her paper and a few telephone calls, she came up with these facts about her southern Minnesota town's rental market:

GROSS RENT MULTIPLIER

MFD VALUE: $100,000   RENTS: $225   UNITS: 4   GRM: 111
MFD VALUE: $310,000   RENTS: $240   UNITS: 12   GRM: 108
MFD VALUE: $185,000   RENTS: $210   UNITS: 9   GRM: 98
MFD VALUE: $800,000   RENTS: $255   UNITS: 28   GRM: 112
AVERAGE MFD GROSS RENT MULTIPLIER IN THIS AREA: 107

In other words, typical rents for apartments in this area could be found by dividing the market value by about 107. Better yet, the market value could often be found by multiplying the monthly rents by the number of units, then by the MFD GRM of 107.

By coming up with this GRM, Cherie was able to quickly pass over unprofitable buys and zoom in on the best opportunities for her investment dollar.

You can do the same.

Using Your New GRM to Make Substantial Profits

The Simpsons came up with an MFD GRM for their area of 100. With it they realized that if they could earn a specific rent with the units by the end of the year, they would easily reach their goal for WEALTH STAGE 3.

First, they double-checked their purchase price. They multiplied their current rents of $200 a month by the eight units and then by the GRM of 100 for a total of $160,000—exactly what they paid for the units.

Next they estimated that they would need another $48,000 in equity, less expenses, to reach their goal. That would mean their MFD-1 would have to be worth about $208,000 at the end of WEALTH STAGE 3. $208,000 divided first by the 100 GRM, then by the eight units gave them a monthly rent per unit of $260. In other words, when they could earn $260 a month per unit the complex would be worth about $208,000 and they would have an Accelerated Equity of $48,000. Great theory, but would it work?

It did. Within one year the Simpsons made a number of Selective Improvements that—combined with normal appreciation and rent increases—earned them a fair market rent of $260 per month per unit. Now they not only had built their first MFD to a value of over $200,000, but they were also able to substantiate the market value with their accurate Gross Rent Multiplier.

How to Keep Uncle Sam Out of Your Pocket

How would like to *legally* defer your taxes until later—or never have to pay them at all?

Real estate exchanging is one of the few ways you can use the government's tax money *legally* for years and not go to jail—in fact they *encourage* you to do it. It's called a "tax-free exchange" and this is how it works:

The Internal Revenue Service says that a gain or loss from the holding of a property is *not taxable* in an exchange of similar properties until the final property in the exchange is sold.

Stu C. estimated that he owed as much as $42,000 in taxes from the growth in equity—the capital gain—in a property he had owned for six years. He knew that the minute he sold this $300,000 property, the IRS would grab *thousands of dollars* in profits off the top as capital gains tax. At my suggestion, Stu took his problem to an accountant. The accountant advised him to do exactly as I told him—and what I'm telling you—about exchanges. He soon exchanged his equity for equity in another MFD before he decided to cash in his chips in 20 years and pay the government the taxes when he's in a lower retirement tax bracket. At that time his taxes will be much less.

The term "tax-free" is misleading. This type of exchange is better called a "tax-deferred" exchange. You must still pay the taxes on the gain, but you may do it when you're in a lower tax bracket and can keep many more dollars.

How to Tally Your Profits from Wealth Stage 3

The Simpsons decided to exchange their equity in MFD-1 for equity in a larger unit. I'll show you exactly how they did it—and how you can do it—in the next chapter. Right now, let's total their net worth at the end of WEALTH STAGE 3:

Original Price		$160,000
Equity Gains		
Creative Purchasing	-0-	
Accelerated Equity—Selective Imp.	$ 25,000	
—Appreciation (12%)	$ 19,200	
Productive Marketing	$ 3,800	
Total Equity Gains		$ 48,000
Current Value		$208,000
Less Down Payment (on purchase)	$ 7,600	
Closing Costs (on purchase)	$ 5,400	
Mortgage Balance	$146,320	
Cost of Selective Improvements	$ 5,900	
Closing Costs (on exchange)	$ 4,160	
Sales Commissions (on exchange)	$ 10,400	
Total Costs		$179,780
TOTAL PROFITS FROM EXCHANGE OF MFD-1		$ 28,220

Now let's add this profit to what the Simpsons started WEALTH STAGE 3 with:

SWITCHING TO MFDS

Equity at the beginning of WEALTH STAGE 3	$43,008
Profit from exchange of MFD-1	$28,220
TOTAL EQUITY AT THE END OF WEALTH STAGE 3	**$71,228**

That's right. Kevin and Dianne Simpson actually built their wealth from $8,000 to over $71,000 in just three short—but profitable—years. Actually, their equity was closer to $80,000 counting the equity gain from appreciation in SFR-4 in the past year. They still own it.

You can do even better. Whether your personal financial goal calls for WEALTH STAGES of three months, a year or even two years, you can *multiply your equity* quickly and easily with the REAL ESTATE MILLIONAIRE PLAN.

10

*Increasing Your Net Worth
with Accelerated Equity Techniques*

    Everyday it's easier to build your wealth with the REAL ESTATE MILLIONAIRE PLAN.
    Everyday you're using new techniques for turning your dollar bills into hundred and even thousand dollar bills.
    Everyday you're learning how other smart investors much like yourself have started with little or no capital and built their fortunes to $100,000, $250,000, even $1,000,000 and more.
    Everyday you step closer to realizing your own goal—whether it's making $50,000 in one year, $1,000,000 in ten years, $300,000 in four years, or, as this book suggests, a quarter million dollars in just five years.
    Today is going to be even better than yesterday because today you're going to learn some of the smart money techniques that have turned hundreds of otherwise average people into *real estate millionaires*. Today is *your* day.

How Smart Real Estate Investors Trim These Two Major Costs

Other than debt-service—the paying off of your mortgage—the two largest expenses you'll have in operating your Residential Income property are:

- Vacancy costs
- Management costs

In the typical RI these costs can total between 10 and 15 percent of your gross rental income each month. Smart REMAP investors know how to cut these costs to a minimum and spend the money on other worthwhile things—like themselves.

Here's how *you* can.

Build Your Bank Account by Cutting Vacancy Costs

The cost of having too many rental units vacant at one time can be staggering. Here's an example: Harold W. owned a 16-unit complex that rented at $225 a unit. His monthly rental income was $3,600. The payment on his mortgage was $2,527 a month. Management costs were about $250 a month. Insurance and other expenses totaled another $120 a month. So his positive cash flow was about $700 a month when all units were full.

Harold went on vacation during August and left the management to one of his older tenants. When he came back from his restful holiday, he found that four of his tenants had taken the opportunity to move out and two others had not paid their rents since he left. His income was down $1,350 *that month.* He had a negative cash flow—he had to feed his investment—of more than $650. It was a pretty expensive vacation.

What could Harold do to ensure himself against loss from vacancy? What can you do? Take these tips from the smart investors who refuse to lose money:

- *Demand a security deposit.* Experienced landlords know that the best way to ensure that tenants will not skip out with back rents due is to demand a security deposit at the time they move in. Harold W. soon set one up that is used by many landlords: first and last month's rent in advance, plus a refundable damage deposit. He loses some potential tenants with this policy, but the ones he has are dependable and usually stay longer.

- *Keep rents competitive.* One major reason why tenants move to other units is to cut expenses. If your rentals are overpriced compared to other rentals in the area, you could lose many valuable rental dollars to vacancies. Keep an eye on the market.

- *Keep units in good repair.* Landlords lose millions of dollars each year in vacancy costs because they don't spend a few extra dollars on the small things that keep their tenants happy: repair dripping faucets, repaint units on a regular basis, have carpets cleaned periodically. Harold began collecting the rent in person. This gave him an opportunity to ask tenants if there were any problems and to see the inside of the units on a regular basis.

Harold learned what hundreds of other smart RI investors have learned: a happy tenant is a profitable tenant. Today, Harold's vacancy factor is almost 0 percent and he is confident that he can leave on a month's vacation and come back to a full house.

Save Thousands of Dollars Every Year by Cutting Management Costs

The other major cost to the RI landlord is management costs—the expenses of having someone keep an eye on your property, collect rents and pay bills as they come due. Normal management costs range from 5 to 10 percent of the gross rent. The REAL

ESTATE MILLIONAIRE PLAN can show you how to put some or all of this cost back into your pocket.

- *Cut collection costs.* Many smart MFD owners cut the cost of collecting rents by setting up a post office box for rents to be mailed to, giving tenants billing envelopes to send their payments in and marking these envelopes with two figures: the rent payment if made on time and the rent payment if made 10 days late. As an example, Barbara L. had hers marked "$250 on the first or $275 on the 15th." This extra 10 percent charge not only deterred late payments, but also helped her with bad checks and skips. The post office box also kept tenants from coming by her house. She saved hundreds of dollars a year with this technique.

- *Evict the live-in manager.* Unless your MFD complex has more than 20 units, you're better off without a live-in manager. Most are paid with free or greatly reduced rent. When Robert S. purchased his six-unit complex, the manager was living in one of the units rent free for managing it. This cost the owner 1/6th or over 16 percent of his rental income. He politely moved her out and moved a paying tenant in.

- *Manage your own complex.* If your unit is large enough to have a live-in manager, why not move in and be your own manager? You will not only be able to keep a better eye on your investment, but you will also qualify for a better loan or refinance.

You can cut your management costs *in half* or less by using these techniques for profitably managing your new MFD.

How to Sell Now—Pay Taxes Later

In the last chapter I teased you with a small amount of powerful information on highly profitable tax-deferred exchanges. This concept may be one of the most important techniques in the REAL ESTATE MILLIONAIRE PLAN, so I'm going to show you more of what it is and how you can make it work for you.

The tax-deferred exchange is a legal method by which owners can exchange their equity in one property for equity in another property *without paying taxes*. The government actually encourages you to keep the tax money, reinvest it and use it for your own good, then pay them later when the value of the dollar and your total tax bill won't be as high. Sound fantastic? It's true.

The tax-deferred exchange is often used by the smart investor—large or small—who has a large equity in an income property that would require a huge tax payment if the property was sold. I'll give you an example in a minute.

First, let's talk about what is called "boot." Boot is the cash or other property received in an exchange to balance the equities.

Here's how it all goes together.

How the Simpsons Exchange Equities Profitably

Kevin and Dianne Simpson were ready to sell MFD-1 and pay taxes on their capital gain when their Realtor, Don, told them about tax-deferred exchanges. They were very interested. After they understood the basics of exchanges, as you do, he showed them two opportunities that they might be able to exchange equities with.

Opportunity L was a 20-unit complex in a good location. The units were two bedroom apartments renting for $200 a month each. The vacancy factor was 5 percent and rising slowly. The management factor was over 11 percent because the live-in manager received free rent *plus* $250 a month. The price was $400,000. The seller had recently "skimmed the cream" by refinancing his property. The current mortgage was $300,000.

Opportunity M was a 16-unit complex with slightly smaller two bedroom units renting for $210 a month. Tenants were primarily college students with high vacancy during the summer months. Damage was also higher than normal. The price was $320,000 with an underlying mortgage of $85,000.

The Simpsons used their GRM to see if rents and value corresponded. With an MFD GRM of 100 they discovered that Opportunity L was priced right at $400,000, and that Opportunity M should be priced at $336,000. The rents on this opportunity were misleading. They estimated that fair market rent on these units should be $200—which gave them a fair market value of $320,000. That's exactly at the asking price.

Comparing Exchanges Profitably

Both opportunities seemed acceptable on the surface, but the most important factor in an exchange is the amount of equity and boot traded. Don filled out this *Exchange Comparison Sheet* to decide on the best tax-deferred exchange:

EXCHANGE COMPARISON

	MFD-1	OPPORTUNITY L	OPPORTUNITY M
FAIR MARKET VALUE	$208,000	$400,000	$320,000
CURRENT MORTGAGE	$146,320	$300,000	$ 85,000
OWNER'S EQUITY	$ 61,680	$100,000	$235,000
BOOT TO BALANCE		($ 38,000)	($173,320)

This sheet told the Simpsons that to exchange their MFD-1 with Opportunity L they would have to come up with about $38,000 in additional cash or "boot," and over $173,000 to exchange with Opportunity M. Don told them that this "boot" was any cash or other personal property—including net mortgage relief—received by the taxpayer in a so called "tax-free" or tax-

INCREASING YOUR NET WORTH

deferred exchange. Their capital gain on which they would have to pay taxes was actually limited to the boot they received.

Don further explained that the *net mortgage relief* is the amount that their mortgage decreases when they exchange properties. In the case of Opportunity L, their mortgage would go from $146,320 to $300,000—definitely not a mortgage relief. In an exchange with Opportunity M, their mortgage would go from $146,320 to $85,000 and they would have a net mortgage relief of about $61,000—taxable as a capital gain.

He reminded the Simpsons that even though they wouldn't have to pay taxes yet on a mortgage exchange with Opportunity L, the seller would still have to pay taxes on the boot of $38,320 in cash he would receive from them—and he may not like to do that.

Working Out the Terms of a Tax-Deferred Exchange

Then Dianne suggested that, rather than pay the owner of Opportunity L a cash boot, they offer him a boot of equity from SFR-4 which they still owned.

Don estimated the current market value of SFR-4 at $55,950 and deducted the existing mortgage of $39,000 to show the Simpsons an equity in SFR-4 of $20,950. He added this to their equity in MFD-1 for a total exchange equity of $82,630. This meant that they would only have to come up with $17,370 in cash, plus closing costs, to exchange MFD-1 and SFR-4 for Opportunity L worth $400,000.

The Simpsons estimated that they had enough cash in their Breeding Fund to pay the boot and closing costs, but they wanted to keep a reserve in it so they asked Don to take his commission on the deal with a note and second mortgage. He agreed.

How to Use a Profitability Checklist

Before Don wrote up the Offer to Exchange, Kevin and Dianne used this *Profitability Checklist* to ensure that the opportunity was an excellent one. You can use this checklist, too, in reviewing your opportunity.

- *Is this a Property with Potential?* Have you used your Cap Rate to make sure this opportunity will give you the return you want? Have you checked to make sure that the seller's statements are accurate? Does your GRM tell you that fair market rents and the market value are in line with other RIs in your area?

- *Are you using Imaginative Financing?* Are you using the Power of Leverage to create a high Leverage Ratio? Are you earning the highest return on Rented Money?

- *Are you using the principles of Creative Purchasing?* Have you planned your presentation to the seller to ensure that you have all the facts you need and can offer them in the most persuasive order? Do you plan to use the See-Saw technique of negotiation to get the best deal for yourself? Do you have valuable concessions that you can relinquish to the seller if necessary?

- *Will you be able to Accelerate Equities for higher profits?* Do you know what Selective Improvements you can make profitably? Is this opportunity in an area of high appreciation? Will tenants' rent more than pay your mortgage to earn an equity build-up?

- *Will you add to profits with Productive Marketing?* Do you plan to make your property easy to sell and easy for someone else to buy—even before you own it? What terms can you sell it on to make it easier to buy? Will you sell for cash, on contract, refinance or exchange?

How Ray B. Saved Thousands of Dollars

Ray B., a machinist, was ready to purchase a 24-unit complex when I showed him a similar Profitability Checklist. Because of it he saved himself thousands of dollars in lost profits—and dozens of headaches.

Ray's opportunity offered him a Property with Potential, Imaginative Financing and Creative Purchasing possibilities, but—he soon realized—couldn't offer him the Accelerated Equity he wanted and needed. The complex was brand new and all of the units were rented at or slightly above fair market rents due to a heavy advertising campaign set up by the builder. After hitting this snag in the REAL ESTATE MILLIONAIRE PLAN steps, Ray backed off the opportunity and began looking for another one.

If he had purchased the unit he would have waited more than a year to see the units appreciate and there were no Selective Improvements he could have made in the meantime. If he had purchased it then sold it a year later he would have not only not made a profit, but he would have lost the closing costs.

Instead, Ray used his Profitability Checklist to decide on the *right* and the *wrong* opportunities.

Taking Over a $400,000 MFD

The offer to exchange equities was accepted by the owner of Opportunity L, and the Simpsons now held title to MFD-2—a $400,000 20-unit apartment complex with a monthly rental income of $4,000.

From their first day they began thinking about the day at the end of WEALTH STAGE 4 when they would again cash in their equity. Their goal for WEALTH STAGE 4 was to reach a net worth of $128,000 and they could now see that it would be easy.

The first thing the Simpsons did when they took title was to give the current manager notice. Between her free rent of $200 a month and the $250 a month that the previous owner was giving her, the management costs were too high for the complex—over 11 percent. The vacancy factor was also climbing steadily. Dianne felt this was because the current manager was slow about collecting rents. She waited until they were one or two months behind before she called the previous owner, who would then evict the delinquent tenants.

Next, they found an experienced apartment manager who would manage the units for a specific fee—5 percent of the month's rental income. That meant that if she kept the 20 units rented she would get her own rent free. She and her husband were also hired at $4 an hour to help with Selective Improvements and specifically ordered repairs. This arrangement worked out well with both the Simpsons and the new manager, Mrs. L.

Setting Profitable Tenant Guidelines

To make your Multi-Family Dwelling profitable you need:

- The highest income
- The lowest expenses

The highest income possible can be earned by making sure that your units are rented at the most competitive rents in your area. They must be high enough to be profitable, yet low enough to attract tenants from other units. Your vacancy factor must be low and your monthly rental income high.

To keep your expenses down you must watch your management costs, unprofitable repairs, mortgage rates and damages.

The fixed income and expenses—such as mortgage rates, management costs and utilities—are difficult to change. The biggest variable in the operation of a Residential Income property is the tenant. He can make the difference. Good tenants can help you with equity build-up, appreciation, Selective Improvements and other profitable factors. The bad tenant can lose you thousands of dollars before you finally get him removed. It's not right that one bad tenant can ruin it for the landlord and the other tenants, but it's a fact of RI ownership. The best thing you can do about it is screen your tenants thoroughly before they move in.

INCREASING YOUR NET WORTH

Here are some guidelines for MFD tenants set up by one of the most successful RI owners on the West Coast: Jerry W. Jerry has three basic understandings with his prospective tenants:

- Tenancy in units is on a month-to-month agreement. Tenants may leave or the manager may request tenants leave with a 20 day notice.
- A damage deposit is necessary and rules on paying for damages will be strictly enforced. No pets.
- The units are rented to both singles and families. No loud noises after 10 p.m. and undue disturbances at any time will be cause for immediate eviction.

Beyond these terms, Jerry expected every tenant to treat the complex as they would if it were theirs. And if they didn't respect other people's rights and property, he evicted them as quickly as he legally could in order to save the cost of future problems and damages. Jerry was polite, firm and very successful.

Cashing In with Productive Marketing

At the end of WEALTH STAGE 4 you're ready to turn your paper profits into *cash*. You want to squeeze every last drop of profit out of your opportunity.

To ensure yourself the largest profit you can do these things:

- *Increase rents to fair market value.* Make sure your rents are competitive with similar units. Sally G. found that the rents on her units were $15 under the market. She felt that $15 each for her six units wouldn't make much difference in the value, but I showed her the Gross Rent Multiplier of 120 for her area that said she was cheating herself out of *$10,800 in equity* by renting the units too low. She quickly raised them before she sold the complex at a healthy profit.
- *Increase tenants.* Never sell an MFD that isn't completely full. Always make sure that your ten-

ants will be staying for at least a few months before you ever decide to put your units up on the market. A complex with a high vacancy factor tells prospective buyers that something is wrong with the complex and it invites them to make cut offers.

- *Improve your image.* Give your units some touch-up paint, clean carpets with heavy traffic, have a gardener cut the lawn more often. Make your opportunity look appealing to the buyer. You can also improve your image by promoting your MFD complex with an interesting name or image. Nat V. used Productive Marketing to increase his profits by naming his complex "Le Chalet" and painting the exterior in creme with brown trim. The extra touch made it more unique than others in the area and commanded $5 a month more rent from the 24 units—an increase in value of $12,000 with a unique PM idea.

How Kevin and Dianne Refinance Their MFD

At the end of WEALTH STAGE 4, the Simpsons were ready to count their winnings thus far. First, they had to pull their equity out of MFD-2. In order to keep the tax-deferred status they earned with the exchange of MFD-1 for MFD-2, they would either have to make another exchange or refinance. They decided that refinancing was the best move. They could keep title to the very profitable property, keep their tax deferred status and pull much of their equity out of MFD-2.

With a complete package in hand, including

- Certified appraisal
- Complete financial books
- Profit and Loss Statement
- Mortgage papers
- Photos

INCREASING YOUR NET WORTH

Kevin and Dianne Simpson approached the mortgage broker who made the loan on MFD-1 two years earlier. They made application for an 80 percent loan on the new value of $530,000 (based on the appraisal and rents of $265 a month per unit).

Within two weeks the mortgage broker called the Simpsons at home and told them the refinance was approved. After paying off the underlying mortgage of $298,200, the Simpsons received a check for the balance.

Here's how the Simpsons totaled up their equity at the end of WEALTH STAGE 4:

Original Price		$400,000
Equity Gains		
Creative Purchasing	-0-	
Accelerated Equity—Selective Imp.	$ 70,000	
—Appreciation	$ 56,400	
Productive Marketing	$ 3,600	
Total Equity Gains		$130,000
Current Value		$530,000
Less Down Payment—Equity in SFR-4	$ 20,950	
—Equity in MFD-1	$ 61,680	
—Cash "boot"	$ 17,370	
Closing costs (on exchange)	$ 8,000	
Mortgage balance (assumption)	$298,200	
Cost of Selective Improvements	$ 12,950	
Refinance Costs (1% loan fee)	$ 4,240	
Total Costs		$423,390
TOTAL PROFIT FROM REFINANCE		
OF MFD-2		$106,610

Let's add in their previous equity:

Equity at the beginning of WEALTH STAGE 4	$ 71,228
Profit from refinance of MFD-2	$106,610
TOTAL EQUITY AT THE END OF WEALTH STAGE 4	$177,838

That's right. The Simpsons passed their goal of making $128,000 by the end of WEALTH STAGE 4 by nearly $50,000—over 38 percent. More than that, Kevin and Dianne built their

Breeding Fund of just $8,000 by over 2200 *percent* in just four short years.

They did it with the same easy-to-use investment tool that's available to you—the REAL ESTATE MILLIONAIRE PLAN.

11

Reaching Your Financial Goal with the Real Estate Millionaire Plan

This is it!

If you've been following my suggested plan for making your first quarter million in real estate in five years, you've reached the most profitable plateau of all—WEALTH STAGE 5.

In this chapter you'll see our friends, the Simpsons, reach their final goal and build their Breeding Fund to over $250,000 in five short years. You'll also see how many other wise investors have used the REAL ESTATE MILLIONAIRE PLAN to build their wealth to $150,000, $300,000, $500,000 and more in a short time.

Most important, you'll see how *you* can reach your own wealth goal quickly and easily with my REAL ESTATE MILLIONAIRE PLAN.

How Successful Investors Find Property with Potential

Now that you are successfully applying the REAL ESTATE MILLIONAIRE PLAN and turning dollars into *thousands of dol-*

lars, you'll find Property with Potential much more easily. In fact, as property owners in your area learn that you are a successful investor, you'll find many of them bringing their opportunities to you. This is when the *big profits* are really made.

But smart RI investors don't wait for opportunities to come to them—they make them. They set out a *Trap Line* much as a trapper would. It works like this:

George H. had more leads on opportunities than he could handle because he set up a Trap Line in his town. He began by going to the people in town that might hear of special real estate opportunities—

- Bank loan officers
- Welcome Wagon owners
- Moving company salesmen
- Courthouse employees
- Newspaper reporters
- Barbers and beauticians
- Appraisers

and asking them to watch for such opportunities for him. He would cultivate their friendship, take them to coffee or lunch periodically and make sure that if they heard anything worthwhile in real estate opportunities they would call him first.

George's Trap Line paid off many times with leads on special opportunities that made him thousands of dollars. You can do the same by cultivating friendships with people who have access to records or who serve people and are in a position to know what's going on in your town or area.

Using the Telephone to Pick Up Big Opportunities

One of the most profitable inventions in the world is the common telephone. With it you can save many days and hundreds of profit dollars as you communicate with buyers and sellers. You can double-check profit-making information almost instantly. You can

REACHING YOUR FINANCIAL GOAL

negotiate large real estate transactions. You can build your fortune more easily with the telephone.

Here's how one highly successful REMAP investor turned his telephone into a money-making device that helped him find Property with Potential.

John T. would place an ad in his local newspaper reading:

> PRIVATE PARTY wants older apartment complex for investment. 6 to 20 units in good condition. Call 555-9138.

John's ad always drew a number of opportunities. Being a smart investor, John prepared a list of questions he wanted to ask sellers and put them by the phone.

- How many units in your complex? Bedrooms? Square feet per unit?
- How old is the complex?
- What are the current rents?
- What is your vacancy factor?
- When was your last rent increase?
- Who are the legal owners?
- Are there any liens or mortgages against the property? How much? To whom? Are they assumable?
- Why are you selling?
- Are there any other reasons?
- May I have the legal description of the property? The address?

Then John would order a Customer Service Package on any properties that sounded interesting. He wanted to verify the facts the seller offered, *plus* get information on the history and price of the property.

Finally, John made appointments to inspect the best real estate opportunities. With this telephone technique John was able to build his personal fortune from $4,500 to over $700,000 in six years.

You can, too. Your success with the REAL ESTATE MILLIONAIRE PLAN has earned you the opportunity to build your fortune quickly and easily because you know how to apply the methods and techniques that can make the difference between working hard and working smart.

How a Smart Investor Can Use Imaginative Financing to Pick Up Bargains

One advantage you now have over other investors is experience. With your own successes and with the examples of success you've read about in this book, you know how to turn opportunities into *cold cash*. This is especially true with Imaginative Financing. Whether you're planning your first transaction or your twenty-first, you can learn profitable lessons in Imaginative Financing from other successful real estate investors.

Smart investors know how to turn other people's misfortune into their own fortune quickly and honestly. They know that many special real estate opportunities are available from:

- Foreclosures
- Tax sales
- Divorce sales
- Estate sales
- Company transfers

They know that these distress sales offer them an opportunity to help others and help themselves. They can give sellers the quick cash they need while they build extra profits for themselves.

Here's how the Simpsons did it.

How Two Investors Turn a Failure into a Success

The Simpsons had just returned from a vacation in the Hawaiian Islands when they received a call from their Realtor, Don, telling them of a distress sale that they could quickly turn into profits.

REACHING YOUR FINANCIAL GOAL

The opportunity was Opportunity M that they had considered exchanging with a year earlier. It was a 16-unit complex with an asking price of $320,000. Rents were $210 a month even though the Simpsons felt that $200 would be more competitive. They had turned down this opportunity because it would have taken them a boot of as much as $173,000 to exchange equities.

Don informed them that the sellers were now desperate to sell because the property had a number of liens against it and creditors were threatening to take the property over. Also, the vacancy factor was over 15 percent and climbing.

The Simpsons smelled a bargain.

Making Sure an Opportunity Isn't a Red Herring

Don ordered a Customer Service Package from a local title company to double-check the facts given to him by the sellers of Opportunity M. They were correct. There were $155,000 in recorded liens against the property, including an $85,000 first mortgage—much of it in default. Creditors were beginning to worry and were considering taking over title to the property in payment.

Don called some of the creditors to decide whether they expected to take action against the property soon. They were considering it, but would prefer that the loans were paid off by the next owner—or at least assumed by someone who would keep them current. Don had an idea.

Using Imaginative Financing to Put Together a Profitable Opportunity

Don quickly scratched out these facts:

Value	$320,000
Less Mortgages and Liens	$155,000
SELLER'S EQUITY	$165,000
Less 10% down	$ 32,000
Balance due	$133,000

Then he explained it to the Simpsons. If they could get the property at last year's price of $320,000, they might be able to assume the current debts on the property with 10 percent down and a note due to the seller in a year or two for the balance. This was Imaginative Financing.

Kevin and Dianne agreed with the method, but asked Don to make the offer at $300,000 instead. The offer was written like this:

> PURCHASE PRICE SHALL BE $300,000. PURCHASER AGREES TO PAY $30,000 DOWN, INCLUDING EARNEST MONEY, AND AGREES TO ASSUME AND PAY RECORDED LIENS ON SUBJECT PROPERTY TOTALING APPROXIMATELY $155,000 ACCORDING TO THEIR OWN TERMS AND CONDITIONS. BALANCE OF $115,000 SHALL BE DUE AND PAYABLE WITHIN ONE YEAR OF CLOSING AND SHALL INCLUDE INTEREST AT THE RATE OF NINE PERCENT PER ANNUM.

Don presented the offer to the sellers who initially resisted both the sales price and the terms of the one year note. Using Creative Purchasing techniques, Don persuaded the sellers that the alternative to this offer was having their creditors confiscate title in payment of liens and mortgages against it. They had no other offers. He made up a Seller's Net Sheet showing them the exact number of dollars they would profit from the transaction.

They were convinced. The sellers signed the Purchase and Sale Agreement that afternoon and—after notifying creditors and getting their approval—the Simpsons now owned MFD-3.

Using Productive Marketing Techniques to Accelerate Equity

One of the best things about the REAL ESTATE MILLIONAIRE PLAN is that, after you're familiar with how it works, you can redesign it to fit your own special investment needs.

REACHING YOUR FINANCIAL GOAL

- *You can combine PWP and IF* as the Simpsons did to find the right opportunity based on smart financing.
- *You can mix CP and PM* profitably and purchase a property in a manner that will help you sell it quickly and profitably.
- *You can use PM to build AE* and find easy profits with both REMAP steps.

Here are some examples:

- Carol J. combined PWP and IF for bigger profits by searching for the best opportunity based on a special financial technique. She discovered that wrap-around mortgages were often the best way to buy PWP with little down and no credit check. With this in mind, Carol made a wrap-around mortgage one of the requirements for any PWP she purchased. She soon found one and used it to help build her fortune by combining REMAP steps.
- Donald F. mixed Creative Purchasing and Productive Marketing by buying his first RI with an FHA loan with a small down. A year later he sold it with the PM technique of offering an easily assumable FHA loan. He received quick cash and high profits by combining CP and PM.
- The Simpsons used Productive Marketing to build Accelerated Equities. By turning MFD-3 into "Senior Villa," they not only cut damages and the vacancy factor, but also added appeal to the units and made the complex more valuable. In doing so they accelerated their equity *and* made the RI easier to market or sell.

Crossing the Finish Line

WEALTH STAGE 5 was nearly over for the Simpsons and they sat down to calculate their net worth—and to review the successes of their five year REAL ESTATE MILLIONAIRE PLAN. They had recently increased the rents at "Senior Villa" to $255 a month to keep up with comparative apartments in their area and computed the new value of MFD-3 on the new rental income.

Their EQUITY SHEET looked like this:

Original Price		$300,000
Equity Gains		
Creative Purchasing	$ 20,000	
Accelerated Equity—Selective Imp.	$ 40,000	
—Appreciation (12%)	$ 40,000	
Productive Marketing	$ 8,000	
Total Equity Gains		$108,000
Current Value of MFD-3		$408,000
Less Down Payment (on purchase of MFD-3)	$ 30,000	
Closing Costs (on assumption)	$ 3,000	
Mortgage and Lien Balances	$277,250	
Cost of Selective Improvements	$ 6,700	
Cost of Productive Marketing	$ 1,800	
Total Costs		$318,750
TOTAL EQUITY IN MFD-3		**$ 89,250**

Now let's add this equity in MFD-3 to their previous equity:

Equity at the beginning of WEALTH STAGE 5	$177,838
Appreciation of MFD-2 during WEALTH STAGE 5 (12%)	$ 63,600
Equity in MFD-3	$ 89,250
TOTAL EQUITY AT THE END OF WEALTH STAGE 5	$330,688

Fantastic!

Kevin and Dianne Simpson's goal was to make their first quarter million in real estate in five years. They actually surpassed that

REACHING YOUR FINANCIAL GOAL

goal by more than *$80,000—over 32 percent*—with their successful application of the REAL ESTATE MILLIONAIRE PLAN.

Their example has been carried through the last five chapters to not only illustrate some of the techniques you can use to build your fortune, but also to prove to you that it can be done. They have shown you the way.

You can set *your* personal financial goal wherever you wish. You can build it in as many WEALTH STAGES as you'd like. You can start with any amount in your Breeding Fund you want—or none at all. You can *succeed* with the REAL ESTATE MILLIONAIRE PLAN.

12

How to Use Advanced Techniques to Make Your First Million in Real Estate in Ten Years

Today, Kevin and Dianne Simpson have nearly reached their *new* wealth goal of $1,000,000.

They still own MFD-2, the 20-unit complex they gained in an exchange, now worth over $600,000. They've since traded the 16-unit MFD-3 for one twice as large—a 32-unit apartment complex valued at more than $900,000. They now control over *1½ million dollars* worth of prime Residential Income property and, as you remember, they started with just a few thousand dollars and the REAL ESTATE MILLIONAIRE PLAN.

You can do even better—because you can learn from the successes and mistakes they and others have made. You can find your Property with Potential sooner, multiply your real estate profits more quickly with Imaginative Financing, use smarter Creative Purchasing techniques to negotiate higher profit deals, Accelerate Equities higher and add even more to your Substantial Profits with the techniques you've learned about Productive Marketing. The Simpsons—and dozens of others—have shown you the way to wealth.

Kevin and Dianne and their two children spent last summer—the whole three months—in Tahiti. They've even considered selling all of their assets and retiring in Tahiti. They know that $1 million will support them like royalty in the South Seas or any other place in the world they choose to go.

They just might do it, too.

How to Cash in on the Real Estate Millionaire Plan

When *that* day comes for the Simpsons, they know how to turn their equity into quick, easy cash.

The REAL ESTATE MILLIONAIRE PLAN is one of the most successful ways of playing the Money Game. The Money Game's objective is to gather as much wealth as you can and trade it for the things you want in life. You start with a small Breeding Fund and, using Rented Money, build your equity until you're ready to "cash in your chips." Then you can use your cashed-in equity to purchase your independence and enjoy life exactly as you wish—without the daily worry of providing the necessities of life.

Here are three ways to cash in the equity you've earned with REMAP:

- Trade Accelerated Equity for More Equity
- Trade Accelerated Equity for Cash
- Trade Accelerated Equity for Annuity

How to Trade Accelerated Equity for More Equity

The first method of cashing in your AE is to continue building your fortune with the REAL ESTATE MILLIONAIRE PLAN by *exchanging* your equity for more Residential Income property. You've reached your financial goal. If you wish, you can trade it for *double* or *triple* that amount. If your goal was to make your first quarter million in five years, you can trade it for a goal of half a million in six to eight years, or even your first million in ten years.

HOW TO USE ADVANCED TECHNIQUES

With an original goal of $100,000 successfully reached, you can trade your equity for $200,000, $500,000 or more with advanced techniques of the REAL ESTATE MILLIONAIRE PLAN you'll soon learn about.

How to Trade Accelerated Equity for Cash

Once you've reached your financial goal with the REAL ESTATE MILLIONAIRE PLAN, you may decide to turn all of your Accelerated Equity into cold, hard cash. You may want to purchase a large home in your favorite part of the country—paying cash for it so you'll never have to make a mortgage payment again. Or you may want the cash to make other investments—or to deposit in the bank and live off the interest.

In any case, you can turn your equity into cash by selling your interest in the RIs you own with one of these methods:

- Sell your RIs for cash proceeds of a conventional loan. In this way you receive the entire sales prices, less costs and debts, in spendable cash.
- Sell your RIs on an assumption where the buyer gives you cash for your equity and takes over your current mortgage payments. Smart sellers will often refinance their property just before they sell it so that the amount the buyer needs to pay to assume the mortgage is lower.
- Refinance your property. By doing this you are getting the best of both—you're receiving a chunk of cash from your equity *plus* you are keeping some equity in a property that continues to grow.

How to Trade Accelerated Equity for Annuity

The most popular—and profitable—method of cashing in on your Accelerated Equity is to turn it into an *annuity* or monthly income for a long period. It's like making a loan where you are the lender. You offer someone else your equity in exchange for a promise of monthly payments from them.

For example, if you held a contract for $250,000 at 9 percent interest for 30 years, you would receive 360 monthly payments of $2,011.60. That's an annuity.

Many smart investors combine the cash and annuity methods of cashing in by trading their Accelerated Equity for a down payment *and* monthly payments.

Sherm V. traded $250,000 of equity in his MFD for $70,000 *in cash* and an annuity of *$1,580 a month* for *30 years* at 10 percent interest.

The advantage of an annuity over cash is the tax savings. If you receive $250,000 in cash at one time, you may be taxed for as much as half of it. But if you take your Accelerated Equity in the form of an installment sale (see Chapter 6), your taxes would only be on the amount you receive *each year*—much lower.

You can use the principle of annuity by selling your RIs on real estate contracts and by investing your own cash in second mortgages.

The REAL ESTATE MILLIONAIRE PLAN is flexible. You can start it with as much or as little cash as you wish—and you can cash in your Accelerated Equity whenever you'd like. You can set your own financial goals and have complete confidence in reaching them when you use the REAL ESTATE MILLIONAIRE PLAN.

How to Use Advanced Real Estate Investment Techniques to Build Your Fortune to a Million Dollars

Now you're ready for ADVANCED REAL ESTATE INVESTMENT TECHNIQUES. The AREITs you will discover in the coming pages have been collected from hundreds of successful real estate millionaires over the past two decades. They are *proven* and they are *profitable*.

Here they are.

HOW TO USE ADVANCED TECHNIQUES

Advanced Real Estate Investment Techniques for Finding Property with Potential

AREIT 1—HOW NOT TO GET TRICKED BY "TENANT STACKING." Some dishonest RI sellers with high vacancy factors will move friends and relatives into units when they put their property on the market in order to make it appear full. Insist on studying the rent rolls and talking with tenants *before* you purchase any Residential Income property. Don't get caught by "tenant stacking."

AREIT 2—HOW TO SAVE HUNDREDS OF DOLLARS BY MAKING YOUR OWN PROFESSIONAL APPRAISAL. You can learn how to appraise your own property with one of the bibles of the appraisal industry, the *Marshall-Swift Residential Cost Book* or *Marshall-Stevens Commercial Cost Book* available from Marshall and Swift Publishing Co., 1617 Beverly Blvd., Los Angeles, CA 90026. These handy guides and supplements will show you exactly how to estimate the cost of any building component-by-component to arrive at a replacement cost—plus show you how to estimate depreciation. You can appraise your own property and save hundreds of dollars with these handy guides.

AREIT 3—GETTING A LOW-COST APPRAISAL FROM THE U.S. GOVERNMENT. For an inexpensive appraisal of your RI's worth, order an FHA or VA appraisal on your property through your lender. The cost is under $100 for SFRs and smaller MFDs. If it's a favorable appraisal, you can use it to substantiate your asking price.

AREIT 4—GETTING PROFESSIONAL ADVICE CAN SAVE YOU THOUSANDS OF DOLLARS. Call in an expert. If you're unsure about the condition of the wiring, plumbing or heating in a Residential Income Opportunity, call in an appropriate tradesman to inspect the unit before you purchase it—or make your offer subject to the inspection. Don't buy surprises.

AREIT 5—HOW TO GET OTHERS TO BRING GOLDEN OPPORTUNITIES TO YOU. Once you've established yourself as a smart REMAP investor, you'll have dozens of professional Realtors asking you to review their property. You're now in the driver's seat. Choose a Realtor that has experience in the type of investments you're making—or who owns RIs himself. Let two or three of the best agents look for opportunities for you. They'll work harder—and make you money.

AREIT 6—MAKING BIG MONEY AT BORING MEETINGS. Many profitable opportunities are discovered at otherwise dull planning commission meetings. Larry E. of Seattle attended one meeting where a zone change was quickly passed for a motel complex in a previously undeveloped area. The next day he approached landowners in the area and picked up one year options on their property. His profits from selling those options during that year totaled *over $500,000*—because he found opportunity where others didn't think of looking.

AREIT 7—USING AN EASY-TO-APPLY YARDSTICK FOR PROPERTIES WITH POTENTIAL. Smart investors always use Gross Rent Multipliers (GRMs) rather than Net Rent Multipliers (NRMs) because different sellers come up with different types of net figures: before debt service, after taxes, before management factors, etc. The GRM is easy to find for any SFR or MFD by dividing the price or value by the total monthly income before expenses. It's an excellent yardstick for checking Properties with Potential quickly and easily.

AREIT 8—WATCHING FOR BALLOON ASSESSMENTS CAN SAVE YOU THOUSANDS OF DOLLARS.

Consider future tax assessments and expected increases when purchasing large properties. A hefty increase in taxes can wipe out your cash flow—especially on highly-leveraged properties. Make sure that a large assessment isn't the reason why the seller is selling. Talk with your local assessor before buying.

AREIT 9—HOW TO KEEP RI UTILITY COSTS DOWN. As a rule, most SFR tenants pay their own heating bills and landlords usually pay the utilities for MFD tenants. If you purchase an MFD, look for one that has individual metering of each unit so you can keep track of tenants who waste utilities—and your money.

AREIT 10—GUARANTEEING FULL OCCUPANCY MAKES SENSE—AND DOLLARS. If the RI you're buying doesn't have 100 percent occupancy, demand that the seller *guarantee* full occupancy for three months or more by putting enough money to cover rents in escrow just in case you can't fill the units quickly. The Simpsons used this technique to earn a $2,400 credit on the closing of MFD-3.

AREIT 11—MAKING SURE YOUR BANK WILL CONSIDER YOUR LOAN. Most new SFRs and MFDs have an economic life of about 50 years. Keep in mind that the banks won't make 30 year loans on RIs with a remaining economic life of just 20 years—unless you can improve the effective age over the actual age of the building by remodeling it. Talk with your banker about loan terms *before* you buy an RI.

AREIT 12—HOW TO MAKE MONEY BY FOLLOWING THE BOOK. Know your local zoning regulations and building codes. For a few dollars you can purchase a copy of each at your local building department. Is your SFR in a zone that will eventually allow an MFD to be built on the property? Could you legally add more units to your MFD in its current zoning? Many real estate millionaires have made extra profits by adding units to existing MFDs because they knew the fine print in their local building and zoning codes.

AREIT 13—BUYING RIs OUT OF SEASON CAN BE PROFITABLE. If possible, buy your RI units in the winter rather than the spring. In the winter you'll see them at their worst, you'll see how effective the heating system is, and you can detect leaks. Also, there is usually a seasonal selling slump in the winter months that makes sellers more motivated. In the spring prices are often inflated and competition for good buys is higher.

AREIT 14—HOW TO GET THE PROFESSIONALS WORKING FOR YOU. Make sure that your banker, accountant, lawyer and Realtor know that you're looking for distress sales or bargains—and that you have the ability to turn them into profits. Each of these professionals comes in contact with many motivated sellers each month and can pass on some excellent buys. Let them know you're interested in finding Properties with Potential.

Advanced Real Estate Investment Techniques for Using Imaginative Financing

AREIT 15—LET THE GOVERNMENT HELP YOU BUILD YOUR REAL ESTATE FORTUNE. The FHA and VA have programs to help eligible investors purchase RIs with low down payments. Investors who plan to live in a unit of their MFD may be eligible for 95+ percent FHA or 100 percent VA loans. Nonowner occupied FHA funds are available for 85 percent loans. Call your local FHA or VA office for more information on this opportunity to use the government's money to help you reach your financial goal.

AREIT 16—FINDING FRIENDS IN HIGH PLACES. Responsive lenders can mean many thousands of dollars in profitable opportunities by making funds readily available to you for worthwhile RI investments. Cultivate lenders as friends and let them cultivate you. After all, you're doing them a service by borrowing money from them, too. Baxter L. used his personal expense account to take his friend, Mark R., to lunch every Friday. Mark, loan officer of a local bank, not only gave Baxter *thousands of dollars* in practical advice in return, but he also approved many of Baxter's RI loans and helped him build his fortune. Mark and Baxter helped each other.

AREIT 17—HOW TO PUT YOUR BEST FOOT FORWARD WITH YOUR BANKER. Prepare your own loan package when you have an opportunity to present it to a lender. Show the loan officer your current financial statement, your projected income, any appraisals done on the property, an outline of your expected SIs and how profitable they will be, plus an outline of how you have used your REAL ESTATE MILLIONAIRE PLAN successfully on other RIs. Be sure to include color photos of the property. You will not only save time for the loan officer, you will also impress him with your professionalism and make it easier for the bank to say "yes."

AREIT 18—HOW TO USE ANNUAL CONSTANTS TO INCREASE LEVERAGE. Many real estate millionaires use *Annual Constants* to estimate loan payoff and increase leverage. The Annual Constant is the total principal and interest payment per year per $1,000 borrowed. Here's an example: the payment due each year on a 20 year loan at 8¼ percent is $103.75 per $1,000—and the annual payment on a 30 year loan at 9¾ percent is $103.87 per $1,000. The annual payments per $1,000 are nearly the same even though the interest rate and payback lengths are different. Smart investors keep the Annual Constant as low as possible so that the amount they pay per $1,000 of Rented Money is low and their leverage is high. To them, the

Annual Constant is more important than the interest rate.

AREIT 19—HOW TO SUCCESSFULLY SPEND TOMORROW'S DOLLARS TODAY. *Present Value of Future Dollars* is also a prime consideration to smart real estate investors. Here's why: today's dollar is always worth *more* than tomorrow's dollar. That's one reason why interest is charged on Rented Money—because the future dollars you pay the lender back with are *less* valuable than the dollars he loans you today. To estimate just how much these future dollars are worth—and compute the actual yield on your investment—you need a table of *Present Value to Future Dollars* available in many mortgage amortization books found in stationery stores. For example, $1 today at an estimated inflation rate of 8 percent per year will only be worth 68 cents in five years and just 46 cents in ten years. Interest charged on a loan takes this into account, plus it adds a percentage for risk and profit. There are many ways a successful real estate investor can use *Present Worth of Future Dollars* tables to make more profitable decisions when buying or selling property.

AREIT 20—MAKING SURE YOU DON'T GET TRAPPED BY ACCELERATION CLAUSES. Watch for *acceleration clauses* in mortgages and contracts. An acceleration clause says that, on certain conditions such as failure to meet payments or pay taxes on time, or on the sale of the mortgaged property, the lender can declare the *entire debt* due and payable. Acceleration clauses are usually used by lenders to discourage assumption of a loan by a purchaser at a rate of interest lower than the current lending rate. Of course, the lender would much rather have his money back and be able to loan it out again at a higher interest rate. If you have any questions on any clause of a mortgage or contract, ask your lawyer to explain it. That's what he's paid for.

HOW TO USE ADVANCED TECHNIQUES

Advanced Real Estate Investment Techniques for Using Creative Purchasing

AREIT 21—HOW TO PROFITABLY BALANCE THE SELLER'S OPTIMISM. In negotiations, the seller is always the optimist. He thinks that his property is the best and the most profitable. He minimizes the repairs that need to be done. He thinks that it's worth much more than a similar property nearby. He feels that all buyers are trying to steal his property. You, as the buyer, must balance this situation by being the pessimist. You see that repairs are going to be extensive and expensive. You expect that there are going to be hidden problems after closing. You estimate that income is actually 20 percent less than the seller says it is—and that the expenses are 20 percent more. Be a skeptical buyer and you won't be disappointed.

AREIT 22—HOW TO WIN THE SELLER TO YOUR SIDE QUICKLY AND EASILY. In preparing for your negotiation session with the seller, make a list of all the points you want to discuss and all of the questions you need answered. Then put these points on a slip of paper in a logical order and keep it near you during negotiations. Most sellers will respect your thoroughness for planning your presentation of the facts. Have all the facts with you when you sit down. Once you have the seller warmed up to sell, don't let him side-step you with a question you can't answer. Set the question aside and politely continue.

AREIT 23—USING SIDE-DOOR CLAUSES TO ENSURE PROFITABILITY IN EVERY DEAL YOU MAKE. Smart real estate investors use as many *Side-Door Clauses* as possible in their Purchase and Sale Agreements or offers. These "contingencies" allow the buyer to step out of an unprofitable deal if he wishes. Here are a few of the most effective ones: "This offer is subject to *satisfactory* financing," or

"This offer is subject to *satisfactory* inspection by _____ (pest inspector, electrician, attorney, partner or other individual)," or "This offer is subject to *satisfactory* verification of income and expenses as represented by the seller." The key word is *satisfactory*. Since it is the *buyer* who must be satisfied, this type of Side-Door Clause offers you a way to ensure the profitability of any deal you make an offer on.

AREIT 24—BIG PROFITS FROM THE SCATTERGUN APPROACH. One successful real estate millionaire, Byron H., had a policy of making low offers on properties that were on the market more than 90 days. He logged property he was interested in in a journal and called the sellers 90 days later to see if it was still available. If so, he made them a low offer. His success ratio is one-out-of-ten, but he makes enough profit on the ones that he does buy to pay for his time and effort—using the Scattergun Approach.

AREIT 25—HOW SMART REAL ESTATE INVESTORS USE THE SUBORDINATION CLAUSE IN BUYING AND SELLING. As you deal with larger parcels of land, you will come across what's called the *Subordination Clause*. It works like this: An SFR or MFD builder buys land on which to build RI units. If he buys on a contract, the seller actually has a "first mortgage" or first right of foreclosure in case of default. Since no intelligent banker will loan money to build on a property where the bank only holds a second mortgage, the buyer should make sure that a Subordination Clause is in the real estate contract he signs with the seller. The clause says that the contract holder, or seller, will subordinate, or move to a second mortgage position, in favor of the development lender. Why should the seller want to give his first position away? Because he knows that his note is more secure with a second mortgage on a fully developed property

HOW TO USE ADVANCED TECHNIQUES

than it is with a first mortgage on raw land. If you're a buyer-developer, make sure you have your attorney put a Subordination Clause in your contract with any seller of land.

Advanced Real Estate Investment Techniques to Accelerate Equities for Higher Profits

AREIT 26—HOW TO "ADD-ON" TO YOUR REAL ESTATE PROFITS. Many real estate millionaires have added thousands of dollars to their fortunes with a simple idea. They increase the value of the RI by adding to its size or *square footage*. They convert unused attic and basement area into additional rentals or storage space that can be rented to tenants. One successful investor, Marty M., broke an older home that was renting for $275 a month into five sleeping rooms with a common kitchen and bath that he rented for $125 a month each—an *increase of $350 a month* in income with a simple modification.

AREIT 27—CUTTING TENANT DAMAGES WITH A SIMPLE CHECK-OUT LIST. To reduce damages to RI units, a number of landlords let new tenants know that they have a check-out list and inspection due before they can get their deposit back. If the tenant knows that the landlord will actually come and inspect the unit before money is refunded, most will be deterred from costly malicious damage.

AREIT 28—ONE SMART LANDLORD FOUND THAT PROMISES CAN BE EXPENSIVE. In handling tenant repair requests, Jim W. found out the hard— and expensive—way to *never promise to fix anything*. If something goes wrong with one of his rentals, he only promises to *check it out* as soon as possible. Some repairs need not be made or are too costly for the benefit derived. In any case, Jim has learned to make an inspection of the problem as soon as possible, *then* decide whether a repair is actually needed.

AREIT 29—HOW TO CUT YOUR INSURANCE COSTS BY AS MUCH AS 50 PERCENT! Once you own a number of RIs, ask your insurance agent for a package insurance policy to cover all of your units. Tyler J. found out that he could save as much as 50 percent on his four RIs by combining them under the same policy with the same agent. He saved *over* $1,000 in premiums the first year.

AREIT 30—REDUCING PROBLEMS WITH SIMPLE RENTAL CLAUSES. Here are some clauses for rental agreements that have been profitable for other smart real estate investors: prohibit animals in MFDs; put a "tax escalation" and "cost of living" clause in your agreements to be able to increase rents as costs increase; require an adequate security deposit to cover possible damage to your units; put in a clause allowing you to show the unit to prospective tenants at reasonable times after formal notice is given to vacate; require tenants to maintain the premises in good repair; do not allow tenants to bring in new tenants to share rent or sublet without your written permission; limit the number of people who may occupy a unit.

Advanced Real Estate Investment Techniques to Add to Your Profits with Productive Marketing

AREIT 31—GETTING PROFESSIONAL HELP CAN PAY OFF. The more equity you build, the more protection you'll want. As you build your first million in real estate, start using the services of your accountant and attorney more. A good attorney will help you review and understand some of the more sophisticated techniques used by buyers and sellers today. Your accountant can save you many times his fee with advice on how to take advantage of legal loopholes in

HOW TO USE ADVANCED TECHNIQUES 215

the tax laws. Remember, you'll soon be paying more taxes as real estate millionaire than you probably made as a salaried worker.

AREIT 32—THREE TYPES OF BUYERS AND HOW TO REACH THEM. Different investors buy RIs for different reasons. Remember this when you're selling your units to another investor. The three basic reasons are: (1) *Accelerated Equity* (appreciation plus Selective Improvements); (2) *Cash Flow* (income greater than expenses); and (3) *Tax Shelter* (depreciation deduction greater than amortization payment). Generally, those starting out in real estate investing are looking for Accelerated Equity, those with high equity prefer Cash Flow income and those who have a large taxable income from other sources are buying for the Tax Shelter benefit of real estate. One of the first questions you should ask a prospective purchaser is "Why do you want to invest in Residential Income property?" His answer will tell you what approach you should use in selling your property to him.

AREIT 33—HOW TO SHOW OFF YOUR PROPERTY'S BEST SIDE. Before you give a prospective buyer a tour of your property, plan your presentation. What are you going to ask buyers to qualify them before time is wasted? How will you actually show them your property? Which units will you show them first? What features will you point out? When and how will you open your books to a qualified buyer? How will you overcome their objections? What words will you use to ask them to make an offer? Do you have Purchase and Sale Agreements handy? Be prepared for success.

AREIT 34—GETTING THE EARNEST MONEY DEPOSIT. Make sure that any offer is accompanied by a substantial earnest money deposit. It should be ½ to 2 percent of the listed price. The more the better. Jack C. took his $160,000 apartment complex off the market for three months on the strength of a $500 deposit. The buyer found another investment, asked for and received a $500 reduction in the down payment from the new seller and promptly forgot Jack. Jack received the full $500 in forfeit, but it was small payment for the time and energy spent with the buyer for three months.

AREIT 35—DON'T FALL FOR THIS BUYER'S TRICK. Many investors give buyers a promissory note for the earnest money "due on closing." Few sellers stop to think what this means. Earnest money paid on the *closing* of a transaction is no security at all. If the buyer defaults and the seller demands his earnest money, the buyer simply tells him that since there was no closing the note is not due. Many sellers don't realize what this type of note means until it's too late and the buyer has tied up their property with *no security*. A promissory note "due on *acceptance* of this offer" is often used when the buyer doesn't want to tie up his cash until the seller actually accepts the offer. Then the earnest money is placed on deposit with an escrow company or real estate broker.

AREIT 36—HOW TO ASK THE RIGHT QUESTIONS OF YOUR BUYER. You'll save thousands of dollars and hundreds of headaches if you learn to qualify your buyers before you spend time and money selling them property. You can quickly qualify their ability and intent by asking these questions: Do you own your own home? Other investments? RIs? How large is your savings? Do you have stocks and bonds? Have you successfully operated RIs before? Which ones? Why did you sell? How do you plan to purchase this unit? Conventional financing? Contract? Assumption and second? Cash? What plans do you have to improve the property? Are they realistic? Why are you buying? Accelerated Equity? Cash Flow? Tax Shelter? How soon can you raise the cash and equity needed? Are you willing to exchange equities? If your buyer feels uneasy telling you about his financial status, suggest that he make a confidential application with his banker who can qualify him for the purchase and advise you.

That's 36 ADVANCED REAL ESTATE INVESTMENT TECHNIQUES to help you build your way from little or no cash to a net worth of over $1 *million* with the REAL ESTATE MILLIONAIRE PLAN. Here are a few ways that other smart investors have modified REMAP profitably.

Other Profitable Applications of the Real Estate Millionaire Plan

The REAL ESTATE MILLIONAIRE PLAN is a proven and successful method of building you wealth with a simple formula:

$$PWP \times IF + CP \times AE + PM = SP$$

Or, PROPERTY WITH POTENTIAL MULTIPLIED BY IMAGINATIVE FINANCING PLUS CREATIVE PURCHASING MULTIPLIED BY ACCELERATED EQUITY PLUS PRODUCTIVE MARKETING EQUALS SUBSTANTIAL PROFITS.

Some real estate millionaires have been successful with modifications of this Plan. They have changed one or more of the REMAP steps to fit their individual needs. You're welcome to use their ideas.

How Sylvan C. Sat Back and Made Money with REMAP

Sylvan C. built his real estate fortune without using the principle of Selective Improvements. Sylvan purchased Single Family Residences in his home town of Milwaukee, put them in the hands of a property management firm to rent them and pay bills for him—and watched his equity grow through *appreciation*. His

$220,000 worth of SFRs appreciated at a rate of about 14 percent a year in his area—an increase of *over $30,000 a year*.

Of course, Sylvan would have had even larger profits if he made Selective Improvements to his units like other REMAP investors, but this system was successful for him and allowed Sylvan to completely forget the problems of being a landlord. Sylvan estimates that, by the time he's ready to retire from his job with the police force, he'll have over $400,000 in equity to cash in and enjoy.

Sylvan modified the REAL ESTATE MILLIONAIRE PLAN to fit his individual needs.

How Bill H. Built His Fortune at Home

Bill H., of San Fernando, California, built his real estate fortune by buying a new home every two years, living in it while he fixed it up, then selling it. His first home was a $9,500 house that he Selectively Improved and sold for $23,950. Number Two was a $34,000 home that he sold two years and many improvements later for $58,500. From there he purchased a 6-unit apartment complex, then traded it for a 20-unit complex and finally moved up to living in his own 42-unit apartment building worth more than $1 million.

Bill lived in and managed each of his MFDs for higher profits. Ten years after he purchased his first home with *no down payment* on a VA loan, Bill controls over a *million dollars* worth of property by simply upgrading his residence.

Most real estate millionaires build their fortunes with SFRs and MFDs that others live in, but Bill found a unique—and profitable—way of taking care of both his shelter and financial needs with the REAL ESTATE MILLIONAIRE PLAN.

How Chet R. Became a Millionaire Handyman

Chet R. always loved fixing things. When he returned to Ohio from World War II he purchased an older home and fixed it up into four apartments, which he quickly rented to returning GIs and their families.

He continued buying older homes near the downtown area and

converting them into rooming apartments that people could afford. He took care of problems promptly and was always fixing up a new unit. Chet made a good living for many years.

Chet always seemed to wear the same old coveralls and very few people ever knew his last name. To everyone he was just "Chet."

Hundreds of people came to his funeral a few years ago—and all were surprised to read in the paper that Chet was a *real millionaire*. A few distant relatives and some local charities were bequeathed the equity he had accumulated, but hundreds of others were given something even greater—Chet's friendship and an affordable place to live.

Chet was a very rich man.

The End of the Beginning

There are dozens of other profitable adaptations of the REAL ESTATE MILLIONAIRE PLAN—and any one of them could take you to your own personal financial goal. The most important secret of REMAP is setting a realistic and attainable goal for yourself, then following the clearly defined steps that will take you to it.

You, too, can enjoy the Good Life and buy your own financial freedom with one of the best—and most needed—investments in the history of mankind: Residential Income real estate. Yes, you can reach *any goal* you realistically set if you apply my easy-to-follow REAL ESTATE MILLIONAIRE PLAN as you've seen it unfold in this book.

Promise yourself today that *you* will soon join the hundreds of successful people who have found happiness and financial freedom with the REAL ESTATE MILLIONAIRE PLAN.

Index

A

Accelerated Depreciation, 104-105, 120
Accelerated equities, 33, 91-107
  appreciation, 103-104
  depreciation, 104-105
  equity payoff, 105-106
  expenses, 98-100
    maintenance, 99
    management, 98-99
    vacancy losses, 99-100
  Packaging, 106-107
  problems, handling, 100
  profitability of rentals, keeping, 96-98
    Cost Method, 98
    Income Method, 96-97
    Market Data Method, 97-98
  profitable renters, finding, 92-94
    Tenants Qualifying Sheet, 93-94
  renter, analysis of nature of, 91-92
  rules, initiating renters to, 94-96
  selective improvements, 101-103
    definition, 101
    interior, 102-103
    in yard, 101-102
Accelerated equity techniques, increasing net worth with, 177-190
  exchange, tax-deferred, 181-183
    boot, 181-182

Accelerated equity techniques, increasing net worth with *(contd.)*
    Exchange Comparison Sheet, 182
    net mortgage relief, 183
    Profitability Checklist, 183-184
    terms, 183
  management costs, cutting, 179-180
  Productive Marketing, 187-188
  refinancing MFD, 188-190
  tenant guidelines, 186-187
  vacancy costs, cutting, 178-179
    competitive rents, 179
    repairs, timely, 179
    security deposit, importance of, 178-179
Acceleration clauses in contracts, watching for, 210
Accountant, using services of, 214-215
Acquisition costs, taxation and, 119
Ad calls, handling, 140-141
Adjusted basis, property sale and, 122
Advanced techniques, how to use, 201-219
  acceleration clauses, 210
  Annual Constants, using, 209-210
  appraisal, professional, making your own, 205
  assessments, awareness of increases in, 206-207
  banker, professional presentation to, 209

Advanced techniques, how to use *(contd.)*
  buyers, three types of, 215
  buying out-of-season, 208
  check-out list and inspection, 213
  "due on *acceptance*" note, 216
  earnest money deposit, 215-216
  economic life, loan and, 207
  exchanging for more equity, 202-203
  FHA and VA programs, 208
  government appraisal, 205
  Gross Rent Multipliers, using, 206
  guarantee of full occupancy, 207
  insurance costs, cutting, 214
  optimism of seller, balancing, 211
  Present Value of Future Dollars, 210
  presentation of property, proper, 215
  professional help, 205-206, 208, 214-215
  questions for buyer, 216-217
  Realtors, using services of, 206
  rental clauses, 214
  Scattergun Approach, 212
  seller, winning to your side, 211
  Side-Door clauses, 211-212
  square footage, adding to, 213
  Subordination Clause, 212-213
  "tenant stacking," avoiding, 205
  trading for annuity, 203-204
  trading for cash, 203
  utility costs, 207
  zoning regulations and building codes, awareness of, 207-208
Advertising property for sale, 113
Agreement closing, 88
Amortizing contract, 72
Annual Constants, using, 209-210
Annuity, advantages of, 204
Appraisal, professional, making your own, 205
Appreciation of property, 103-104
Appreciation from residential income properties, 29-30
AREITs, 204-217 (see also "Advanced techniques. . .")
Assessments, watching for increases in, 206-207
Assets, borrowing from, 62
Associates as source of investment capital, 65
Assumptions of loans, 73
Attorney, using services of, 214-215
Availability of money to investors, 69

B

Balloon assessments, watching for, 206-207
Balloon contract, 72
Banker, preparing loan package for, 209
Boot, meaning of, 181-182
Borrowing collateral, 66-67
Borrowing profitability, 58-59
Breeding Fund, seven ways to build, 61-63
  assets, borrowing from, 62
  loaning money to yourself, 63
  personal property, selling, 62
  real property, selling, 62
  savings, personal, 61
  second mortgage, 63
  signature loan, 62-63
Broker Packaging, 30
Building codes, knowledge of, 207-208
Buyer, property price set by, 50-51
Buyers, three types of, 215

C

Capital, minimal, starting plan with, 36-37
Capital gains, meaning of, 118
Capitalization rate, 165-166
  meaning, 96-97
  and rent, 165-166
Cash, four places to borrow 64-65
  associates, 65
  conventional loans, 64
  credit cards and overdraft accounts, 64
  investors, other, 64-65
Cash, four places to borrow, 64-65
Cash Method of selling property, 113-114
Check-out list and inspection, using, 213
Closing transaction, 88-90
  costs, 89
  in escrow, 89-90
  Prorations, 89
  types, three, 88
Collateralization, 69-70
Community property, 119
Competitive rents, importance of, 179
Component Depreciation, 104-105
Conventional financing, using, 67-68
  mortgage bankers, 67-68
  securing, 68

INDEX

Corporate ownership, 119
"Cost of living" clauses, 214
Cost Method of pricing property, 50-51
Cost Method of determining rents, 98
Counter offers, how to handle, 87
Courthouse records, checking to find seller, 148
Creative Purchasing, 33
Creative Purchasing, using to negotiate, 75-90
   closing transaction, 88-90
      costs, 89
      escrow, 89-90
      Prorations, 89
      types, three, 88
   crossroads risks, 76-77
   definition, 76
   negotiating profitable deal, 86-88
      counter offers, handling, 87
      see-saw techniques, 87-88
   offer, how to make, 79-81
      descriptions, legal, importance of, 79-80
      earnest money, getting, 81
      escrow instructions, 80-81
      price and terms, 80, 81-84 (see also "Terms in offer. . .")
   Plus and Minus Sheet, using, 77-79
      minuses, overcoming, 78-79
      presenting offer to seller, 84-86
   risk, reducing, 76-77
Credit cards, 64
Crossroads risks, meaning of, 76-77
CSPs, 47-48
Customer Service Package, 47-48

D

Dealer or *investor*, differences between, 121
Declining Balance Method of depreciation, 120-121
Depreciation of property, 104-105
   and taxation, 120
      Declining Balance method, 120
      Straight Line method, 120
Descriptions of property, legal, importance of, 79-80
Divorce sales as source of properties, 45
"Due on acceptance" note, 216

E

Earnest money deposit, getting, 81, 215-216
Economic life of property, relationship of to loan, 207
Equity build-up from residential income properties, 29-30
Equity payoff, 105-106
Escrow instructions in Purchase and Sale Agreement, 80-81
Estate sales as source of properties, 45
Exchange, tax-deferred, 122, 173-174, 181-183
   boot, 181-182
Exchange Comparison Sheet, 182
Expenses, keeping down, 98-100
   of maintenance, 99
   of management, 98-99
   vacancy losses, 99-100
Expenses, lower, with MFDs, 163

F

FHA appraisal, 205
FHA insured mortgages, 70
   points, reason for, 70-71
FHA programs, using, 208
Financial closing, 88
Financial goal, reaching with REMAP, 191-199
   Imaginative Financing, 194-196
   property with potential, finding, 191-192
   Trap Line, 192
   telephone, using, 192-194
Financial institutions, checking to find seller, 148
Financing, Imaginative, to get start-up money for investing, 57-74
   availability of money, 69
   borrowing, 58-59
   Breeding Fund, seven ways to build, 61-63 (see also "Breeding Fund. . .")
   cash, four places to borrow, 64-65 (see also "Cash. . .")
   without cash, three methods of starting, 65-67
      borrowing collateral, 66-67

Financing, Imaginative, to get start-up money for investing *(contd.)*
   100% financing, 65-66
     through Real Estate Contract, 66
   collateralization, 69-70
   conventional financing, 67-68
     mortgage bankers, 67-68
     securing, 68
   first property, buying with little cash, 61
   insured mortgages, 70
     points, reason for, 70-71
   leverage, power of, 59-60
   loan-to-value ratio, 68-69
   mortgage, definition of, 68
   qualifying for loan, 60-61
   secrets, 69-70
   types, four, 71-74
     contracts, 68, 71-72 (see also "Land contracts")
     second mortgages, 72-73
     "sweat equity," 73-74
     underlying loan, assuming, 73
     wrap-around mortgages, 72-73
Foreclosures as source of properties, 46
FSBOs as source of properties, 46-47

G

Goal, personal financial, how to find, 35-36
Government, using programs of, 208
Government appraisal, 205
Government survey as legal description, 80
Gross Rent Multiplier, 153-154
   setting for MFDs, 172-173
Growth in equity greater with MFDs, 164
Growth trends in property, how to read, 41-42
Guarantee of full occupancy, demanding, 207

H

Hard Money Mortgage, 115

I

Imaginative Financing, 33
Imaginative financing, using to invest, 57-74 (see also "Financing, imaginative. . .")
   Improvements, making selective, 101-103
   definition, 101
   interior, 102-103
   in yard, 101-102
Improvements on residential income properties, 30
Income Method of pricing property, 50-51
   of determining rents, 96-97
Income Opportunity Fact Sheet, 112-113
Income Property Analysis, 51-52, 54-55
Individual investor, advantages of, 26
Industry, real estate as, 24
Installment sale as method of delaying taxes, 122
Insurance costs, cutting, 214
Insured mortgages, 70
Investors, other, as source of investment funds, 64-65

J

Junior mortgage, using to build investment fund, 63

L

Land contracts, 68, 71-72
   amortizing, 72
   balloon, 72
Landscaping for yard, 101-102
Legal closing, 88
Leverage, residential income properties and, 28-29, 59-60
   greater effectiveness of on MFDs, 164
Leverage ratios, 133-135
Limited partnerships, 119
Liquidity of residential property income, 27-28
Loan brokers, 67-68
Loan-to-value ratio, 68-69

INDEX

Loaning money to yourself to build investment fund, 63
Loans, conventional, 64

M

Maintenance costs, minimizing, 99
Management costs, minimizing, 98-99
   for MFDs, how to cut, 179-180
Market Analysis Method of pricing property, 50-51
Market Data Method of determining rents, 97-98
Marketing, Productive, 109-123
   cashing in, 110-111
   questions to ask, 111
   Ramsey's Rule, 110
   refinancing property, 116-117
      conventional, 116-117
   selling profitably, 111-116
      Income Opportunity Fact Sheet, 112-113
      preparation, 112
      promoting property, 112-113
      records, getting in order, 112
      terms, 113-116 (see also "Selling RI property...")
   tax planning, 117-123 (see also "Tax planning...")
      acquisition costs, 119
      capital gains, 118
      definition, 117
      delaying obligation, 122-123
      interest, 119-120
      operation, 120-121
      origination, 118-120
      ownership, methods of, 118-119
      termination, 121-122
Marshall-Stevens Commercial Cost Book, 205
Marshall-Swift Residential Cost Book, 205
Metes and bounds as legal description, 80
MFDs, 27-28 (see also "Residential income property")
   investments in, 161-175 (see also "Multi-family dwellings...")

"Millionaire plan," building future with 23-28
   capital, starting with minimal, 36-37
   goal, finding personal, 35-36
   how it works, 31-34
      formula, 32
   individual investor, advantages of, 26
   information, availability of, 26
   knowledge, first-hand, 25
   necessity, real estate as, 25
   residential income property, 27-28
      growth, 28
      liquidity, 27-28
      six steps to wealth, 28-31 (see also "Residential income property")
   stages, building wealth through, 34-35
Mortgage, definition of, 68
Mortgage bankers, 67-68
Motivated sellers, search for, 148
Multi-family dwellings, increasing income by investments in, 161-175
   capitalization rate, 165-166
   cash flow, improved, 163-164
   Creative Purchasing techniques, 171-172
   equity growth, 164
   expenses, lower, 163
   GRM, setting, 172-173
   income, higher, 162-163
   money techniques, using, 169-170
   most profitable, 161-164
   negotiating transaction, 171-172
   profitability, checking properties for, 166-168
   profits, tallying, 174-175
   risks, controlled, 164
   tax shelter, better, 164
   taxes, deferring, 173-174
   types, 162

N

National Association of Real Estate Boards, 46
Necessity, prime, real estate as, 25
Negative cash flows, 29

INDEX

Negotiating profitable deal, 86-88 (see also "Creative Purchasing. . . .")
  counter offers, how to handle, 87
  see-saw techniques, 87-88
Net mortgage relief, 183
Net Rent Multipliers, 206
Newspaper ads, learning from, 41
100% financing to purchase property, 65-66

O

Out-of-season buying, 208
Overdraft accounts, 64
Ownership of property, types of, 118-119

P

Packaging, 106-107
  for residential income properties, 30-31
Personal property, selling to build investment fund, 62
Planners, community, learning to consult with, 41
Plants for yard, 102
Plus and Minus Sheet, using, 77-79
  minuses, overcoming, 78-79
"Points" on insured mortgages, reason for, 70-71
Potential tenants, how to check out, 141-142
Preapproved financing, 152-153
Present Value of Future Dollars, using, 210
Preventive maintenance, importance of, 99
Price of property in offer, 80, 81-84
Principal residence, taxes upon sale of, 122-123
Problems, how to handle, 100
Productive Marketing, 33-34
Professional help, importance of, 214-215
Profitability Checklist, 183-184
Profitability of property, verifying, 48-52
Profitability of rentals, insuring, 96-98
  Cost Method, 98
  Income Method, 96-97
  Market Data Method, 97-98
Profitable renters, finding, 92-94
  Tenant's Qualifying Sheet, 93-94
  Property with high potential, how to find, 33, 39-55
  area planners, consulting with, 41

Profitable renters, finding (contd.)
  growth trends, how to read, 41-42
  income and profitability, analyzing 51-52, 54-55
  Income Property Analysis, 51-52, 54-55
  investor, requirements as, 43
  knowledge as potential profit, 42
  newspaper ads, checking, 41
  profitability, verifying, 48-52
    methods of pricing, 50-51
  Property Pricing Sheet, 50, 51, 53-55
  rental properties, profiting from, 40
  title to property, checking, 47
    CSPs, 47-48
  where to find, 43, 45
    FSBOs, 46-47
    realtor, 46-47
Property Pricing Sheet, 50, 51, 53-55
Prorations, responsibility for, 89
Purchase Money Mortgages, 115-116
Purchase and Sale Agreement, 79-81
  descriptions, legal, 79-80
  earnest money, getting, 81
  escrow instructions, 80-81
  price and terms, 80, 81-84
Purchasing power, 75-90 (see also "Creative Purchasing. . . .")

Q

Qualifying buyer by right questions, 216-217
Qualifying for loan, 60-61

R

Ramsey's Rule of Productive Marketing, 110
Real estate contracts, 68, 71-72 (see also "Land contracts")
  as type of Soft Money Mortgage, 115-116
Real property, selling to build investment fund, 62
Realtor, experienced, using, 206
  as source of properties, 46-47
Recapture, meaning of, 121
Records, getting in order to sell, 112
Refinancing property, 116-117
  conventional, 116-117
REMAP, 23-38 (see also " 'Millionaire plan,' building future with")

INDEX

Rental clauses to reduce problems, 214
Rental properties, profiting from, 40 (see also "Property with high potential. . . .")
Renter, analysis of, 91-92
Repairs, timely, importance of, 179
Requirements for home renters, ten, 93-94
Residential income property, 27-28
  growth, 28
  liquidity, 27-28
  six steps to wealth, 28-31
    appreciation, 29-30
    equity buld-up, 29
    leverage, 28-29
    "packaging," 30-31
    selective improvements, 30
    tax savings, 31
Risks, nature of, 76-77
  more controlled in MFDs, 164
Roofing of unit, 102
Rules, initiating renters to, 94-96

S

Savings, using personal, 61
Scattergun Approach, using 212
Second mortgages as type of Imaginative Financing, 72-73
  to build investment fund, 63
Security deposit, importance of, 178-179
See-saw Techniques of negotiating, 87-88
Selective Improvements, making 101-103 (see also "Improvements. . . .")
  cosmentic, 154-155
  in residential income properties, 30
Seller, presenting offer to, 84-86
  winning to your side, 211
Selling RI property profitability, 111-116
  Income Opportunity Fact Sheet, 112-113
  preparation, 112
  promoting property, 112-113
  records, getting in order, 112
  terms, 113-116
    cash method, 113-114
    Soft Money Mortgage, 115-116
    Wrap-Around Method, 114-115
Semlo Investments, 116
SFRs, 27-28 (see also "Residential income property")

SFRs as best first investment, 128-129
  choosing, 129
  Investment Rating Guide, 131-132
Side-Door Clauses, using, 211-212
Signature loan, 62-63
Soft Money Mortgage to sell property, 115-116
Straight Line Depreciation, 104-105, 120-121
Subordination Clause, using, 212-213
Sum-of-the-years-digits method of depreciation, 120
"Sweat equity," 73-74

T

Tax delinquent sales as source of property, 45
"Tax escalation" clauses, 214
Tax planning, profiting from, 117-123
  acquisition costs, 119
  capital gains, 118
  definition, 117
  delaying obligation, 122-123
    exchange, 122
    installment sale, 122
    principal residence, sale of, 122-123
  interest, 119-120
  operation, 120-121
    depreciation, 120-121
  origination, 118-120
    ownership, methods of, 118-119
  on termination, 121-122
    adjusted basis, 122
    dealer or *investor*, 121
    recapture, 121
Tax savings on residential income properties, 31
Tax shelters, 52, 104-105
  superior, in MFDs, 164
Taxes, definition of, 117
Telephone, using profitably, 192-194
Tenancy in Common, 119
Tenant guidelines, setting, 186-187
"Tenant stacking," 205
Tenants, potential, how to check out, 141-142
Tenants Qualifying Sheet, 93-94

Terms in offer to purchase, 80, 81-84
    how to write, 81-84
Title insurance companies, 47
    CPSs, 47-48
Titles to property, checking, 46-47
Transfer sales as source of properties, 46
Trap Line, establishing, 192

U

Underlying loan, assuming, 73
Utility bills, monitoring, 207

V

VA appraisal, 205
VA insured mortgages, 70
    points, reason for, 70-71
VA programs, using, 208
Vacancy costs, how to cut, 178-179
Vacancy losses, reducing cost of, 99-100

W

Wealth stages, building, 126
    ad calls, handling, 140-141

Wealth stages, building *(contd.)*
    and Creative Purchasing techniques, 135-136
    example, 126-144
    leverage, power of, 133-135
        ratios, 133-135
    potential tenants, checking, 141-142
    Productive Marketing, 142-143
    Selective Improvements, making to accelerate equity, 139-140
    SFRs as best first investment, 128-129
        choosing, 129
        Investment Guide, 131-132
Wrap-Around Method of selling property, 114-115
Wrap-around mortgages, 72-73, 151

Y

Yard, making Selective Improvements in, 101-102

Z

Zoning boards, consulting with, 41
Zoning regulations, knowledge of, 207-208